Hemingway or Twain?

Unleashing Your Author Personality

Jeanne Martinson, MA

WOOD DRAGON BOOKS

Hemingway or Twain? Unleashing Your Author Personality
By Jeanne Martinson, MA
Copyright 2015 by Jeanne Martinson
All rights reserved. This book, or parts thereof, may not be reproduced in any form without permission of the author, except for a review

A Wood Dragon Book
www.wooddragonbooks.com
P.O. Box 1216, Regina, Saskatchewan, Canada S4P3B4
Telephone +1.306.569.0388

Library of Canada cataloguing in publication data is available upon request.

ISBN: 978-0-9948700-0-1

CAVEATS

Gender
This book alternates between female and male pronouns, with the male pronouns used in the odd chapters and the female pronouns used in the even chapters.

The Reader
This book was written for the non-fiction author, although many of the concepts will be of value to fiction authors as well.

The Self-Published Author
This book was written for the self-published author, although many of the steps in the process will be of value to authors who pursue a traditional publisher or use an assisted-publishing agency.

DEDICATION

To
P. D. James
(Phyllis Dorothy James)

August 3, 1920
to
November 27, 2014

ACKNOWLEDGEMENTS

When I wrote my first book fifteen years ago, I was blessed to be surrounded by friends, family and colleagues who acquiesced happily to my request to give my book manuscript a glance over and inform me of any areas they thought should be changed. My author ego was fragile and young and I knew that a few of them felt uncomfortable suggesting changes over and above grammar and spelling options, even if they thought their suggestions on content would have improved the book.

It is certainly always wonderful to hear that a reviewer likes your book and sees little room for improvement. However, what an author really needs is a group of critical thinkers whose insights increase the readability and value for the end reader. Fortunately, that is exactly the kind of input given to me by the group below.

To be honest, I am still surprised that my volunteer editors see contributing editorial insight to my books as a privilege, not as a chore. I hope they in turn are not surprised to hear how grateful I am for their contribution.

This book has been MUCH improved by the sharp-eyed skills of Carla McEachern, Laurelie Martinson, Carole Stepenoff, Laurie Gosselin, Pat Dell, I.J. McIntyre and Carolyn Schur. I would particularly like to acknowledge my husband, Malcolm Bucholtz, for his emotional support and editorial suffering through all four drafts.

Lastly, I would like to thank you, my reader, for picking up this book and spending time with these ideas. I hope you find the book pithy and practical.

Table of Contents

Caveats iii
Dedication v
Acknowledgements vii
From the Author xiii

INTRODUCTION

(1) The Four Mental Hurdles to Jump to Get Started 15

SECTION ONE

(2) Hemingway or Twain – The Four Questions 17
(3) Are you an Introvert or Extravert? 21
    Advice for Extraverts 24
    Advice for Introverts 25
    Quiz: Am I an Introvert or Extravert? 26
(4) Are you Pressure-Prompted or Pleasure-Prompted? 29
    Advice for Pressure-Prompted Authors 32
    Advice for Pleasure-Prompted Authors 33
(5) Are you a Linear or a Lateral Thinker? 35
    Exercise: Am I a Linear or Lateral Thinker? 39
(6) Are you an Early Bird or a Night Owl? 41
    Quiz: Am I an Early Bird or Night Owl? 43

SECTION TWO

(7) The Milking Stool of Your Book and Business 45
    Marketer/Entrepreneur 47
    Manager/Administrator 48
    Writer/Author 48
(8) Legacy Publishing, Assisted-Publishing, or Self-Publishing: Author Choice? 51
    Pros and Cons of Legacy Publishing 54
    Pros and Cons of Assisted-Publishing 58
    Pros and Cons of Self-Publishing 59

SECTION THREE

- **(9) The Book Project Model** **63**
- **(10) Step One - Obsess** **63**
  - *Credibility* *64*
  - *Revenue* *65*
  - *Obsession* *65*
  - *Codify Ponderings* *65*
  - Exercise: Step One 67
- **(11) Step Two - Clarify** **69**
  - *Enlightened, Entertained or Educated?* *70*
  - *Geographic location of your Readers?* *71*
  - *Theme and Title?* *72*
  - *Inclusions and Exclusions?* *73*
  - *Structure?* *74*
  - Advice for Asking Others for Input 77
  - Exercise: Step Two 78
- **(12) Step Three - Research** **79**
  - *Interviews with other experts* *80*
  - *Academic Sources* *81*
  - *Client Stories* *83*
  - *Your experiences* *83*
  - Exercise: Step Three 84
- **(13) Step Four – Chunk or Outline** **85**
  - *Surrounded by piles* *86*
  - *Pick a Pile* *87*
  - Exercise: Step Four 88
- **(14) Step Five - Write** **89**
  - Where do you write? 90
  - When and how long do you write? 91
  - Cracking Author's Block 92
  - Exercise: Step Five 95
- **(15) Step Six – Market (Round One)** **97**
  - *Book launches versus book signings* *98*
  - *Book signings* *99*
  - *Book launches* *100*
  - *Media appearances* *101*

Exercise: Step Six 102
(16) Step Seven - Edit **103**
    Content *104*
    Readability *104*
    Impact *104*
    Spelling and Grammar *104*
    Expert Content *105*
  Guidelines for Author-Editor Relationships................................... 106
  Exercise: Step Seven 107
(17) Step Eight – Produce **109**
    Size *110*
    Fonts *110*
    Printing *110*
    Cover Design *111*
  Exercise: Step Eight... 112
(18) Step Nine – Market (Round Two) **113**
    Book signings *114*
    Book launch *114*
    Sales through social media *114*
    Your book as primary marketing piece *115*
    Your book in your pocket *115*
    Cover cards *115*
    Media *115*
    Dripping on your database *116*
    Client Bulk discounts *116*
    Book awards *116*
    Back of the room sales *117*
    More books *117*
  Exercise: Step Nine 118
(19) Step Ten – Repurpose and Reposition **119**
    Articles and blogs *120*
    eBooks *120*
    Audio books and iTunes *121*
  Exercise: Step Ten 122

SECTION FOUR

(20) The Yada Yada 123
(21) The Cover.. 125
    Front cover design... 126
    Spine design 126
    Back cover design 126
    Book content bleep... 127
    Biographic author bleep 127
    ISBN... 128
(22) The Front Pages 129
    Autograph page 129
    Title Page 130
    Copyright page 130
    Acknowledgements 131
    Note from Author... 132
    Caveats.. 132
    Table of Contents... 132
    Early Praise for the book 132
    Dedication 132
(23) The Back Pages 135
    Index... 135
    Information about your business 136
    Previous/upcoming books.. 136
    Biography of the Author... 137
    Bibliography or Resources 137
    Endnotes, footnotes, and notes 137
(24) The End of the Story 139

SECTION FIVE

Index 141
Resources 143
About the Author 145
Books by the Author 147
Author Services 155

FROM THE AUTHOR

Somehow over the past fifteen years, I have muddled my way into three models that affect author success.

The Author Personality is a model of four questions, that once answered, can help an author move forward with minimum stress to complete his or her manuscript.

The Milking Stool model is a play on the antique milking stool I have in my living room. Today, it is only used as a surface to stack books and hold tea cups, but once upon a time it was doing its namesake work at my husband's grandfather's dairy farm. The Milking Stool triangle of legs explains the three essential roles and their accompanying tasks that must be completed to take an author down the writing path to victory.

The third model, the Book Project Model is a step-by-step process that an author can follow to ensure success in launching their book to the world. The steps include: obsess, clarify, research, chunk or outline, write, market edit, produce, market, repurpose and reposition.

When I was struggling with completing my graduate school thesis, a colleague puzzled me with the question: what is the best kind of thesis? The answer: a finished one. My hope for this book is that it will help you, the non-fiction author, to have the best kind of book: a finished one.

Together, the three models within will assist you to imagine and create a great book, while saving time, money and stress.

1

THE FOUR MENTAL HURDLES TO JUMP TO GET STARTED

For busy people, writing a book is a task easily set aside for another day. There is always so much to do; the prospect of taking on a book project is overwhelming. "Perhaps when I go on vacation," we tell ourselves. And so we put it off. P.D. James, a well-known British mystery writer, said "There is never a convenient time to start your first book." That was true for her first book, and it will be true for yours as well.

Perhaps you are waiting for the brilliant idea. Author Stephen King wrote about his source of fiction ideas, "there is no idea dump, no story central ... good ideas seem to come quite literally from nowhere, sailing at you right out of the empty sky; two previously unrelated ideas come together and make something new under the sun. Your job isn't to find these ideas but to recognize them when they show up."

If you are writing fiction, certainly there is something to be said for waiting for and recognizing the brilliant idea. But if you are an expert in a certain field and are writing a book to codify your knowledge and ideas into another medium, King's advice does not necessarily apply. You are surrounded by ideas you have stored on memory sticks, blog sites, in previously published short works and presentation material. As the first hurdle is to accept the time is now, the second hurdle is to realize that you have all the ideas you need.

You want to write a book, you have the material, but how do you go about it? Perhaps you have attended a writing conference or bought several books on writing. You have heard wonderful things about the results of putting your ideas down in a long lasting form. You take your pages and pages of notes home and nothing occurs. You are overwhelmed and stuck. To clear the third mental hurdle, you need to discover that there is more than one way to write a book and you have to make a choice.

You finally decide on a model or process to follow but the project feels like you are swimming against the current. You follow one person's advice and you become frustrated. You switch gurus and models only to find the new suggestions impossible to fit into your work or lifestyle. Whose individual ideas and process do you follow? Or a combination of all?

Many speakers and other experts want to become authors; they recognize there's value in a book, but they just can't seem to get the project moving. The truth of this fourth hurdle is that the right process for each author is the one he designs himself. This book was written to help you create that design so you may manifest your book project with minimum time and stress.

This is the time!
You have all the ideas you need!
There is more than one way to write a book and
you must make a choice!
The right process for you is the one you design yourself!

2
HEMINGWAY OR TWAIN? THE FOUR QUESTIONS

When we read about an author we admire, we say to ourselves, "This is how they do it. This is how they write. This is how they research. This is how they edit. This is how they market. It must be the right way." And then we follow their lead.

A fiction writer may look at Hemingway's success and believe that if she wrote like Hemingway, she too would be that successful. Or, if she adopted Twain's habits, she too would be prolific.

Hemingway wrote standing up, saying that "writing and travel broaden your ass if not your mind and I like to write standing up." Charles Dickens, Virginia Woolf, Lewis Carroll all wrote standing up as well, and the seven foot tall Thomas Wolfe used the top of his refrigerator as a writing desk. However, both Twain and Truman Capote wrote lying down, Capote bragging that he perceived himself "a completely horizontal author".

Both fiction and non-fiction authors have their claims about substances helping or destroying their writing quality and quantity. Twain, who was well known for both his fiction and non-fiction work, wrote daily, smoking 40 cigars. "A bad writing day is when I ran out of cigars before I got that last brilliant thought." Hemingway started drinking at two in the afternoon and we know how that turned out.

We look to our writing heroes for the perfect number of words an author should write in a day. George Bernard Shaw wrote 1000 words per day, Thomas Wolfe 10,000 and Hemingway a mere 500.

Writing style, habits, surroundings, interactions with others and decisions about process all affect our success. As an author, you must ask yourself - whose way of writing are you paying attention to? The only answer should be – your own. The person you should be paying attention to is you.

When authors get stuck on a book writing project, they may be receiving too much advice from too many people and none of it is working for them. An author needs to respect her own style and inner Author Personality so that she can move forward in this adventure with speed and serenity.

Therefore the first step to success as an author is to identify your own Author Personality. By knowing your specific writing preferences, you can avoid frustration and delay as you move through the steps of the Book Project Model (obsess, clarify, research, chunk or outline, write, market, edit, produce, market, repurpose and reposition).

To determine your Author Personality, consider these four distinctions:

1. Are you an introvert or an extravert?
2. Are you pressure-prompted or pleasure-prompted?
3. Are you a linear or a lateral thinker?
4. Are you an early bird or night owl?

Each of these questions affects, to a lesser or greater degree, your success in the different steps of a book writing project. These are four different and separate questions. They do not create an amalgamated model. Knowing even the answer to one of the four will set you free in some ways to be a successful author.

In the next few chapters we will explore each question through the fictional characters of John, Frank, Penny and Georgia. In the latter part of the book, you will see the questions applied to each of the steps of the Book Project Model and come to understand how unleashing your Author Personality can save you pain, time and money.

3

ARE YOU AN INTROVERT OR EXTRAVERT?

John is an extravert and has taken advice from an author coach who has instructed, "You know what you need to do, John? Put all of your research and notes in a couple of boxes, get in your car and drive to a resort where there's no Wi-Fi, television or crowds of people. Concentrate, think and be alone with your muse."

John takes this advice. He gets in his vehicle, drives to the resort. He tells the staff at the front desk, "No calls please, I'm writing." John is in his space. It's quiet, it's serene. Two hours after checking in, he is restlessly pacing the 14 by 14 foot room, his eyes darting left and right as he searches desperately for an escape from his self-imposed exile. He runs his hands through his hair and mumbles, "How will I ever finish this book? Forget finish – how will I ever start!" He sits down on the bed in despair, "I guess I just wasn't meant to be an author."

John is an extravert. By attempting to write as an introvert, he is not respecting his inner Author Personality.

The terms *introversion* and *extraversion* were made popular by Carl Jung in 1921 and have been used in most psychological assessment tools since that time, including the ubiquitous Myers-Briggs Type Indicator (MBTI).

One of the first people to define introversion and extraversion in a psychological context, Jung theorized that each person falls into one of two psychological categories - the introvert or the extravert. Jung compared these two types to the ancient archetypes of Apollo and Dionysus. The introvert is likened to Apollo, who shines light on understanding and focuses on the internal world of reflection, dreams and vision while Jung associated the extravert with Dionysus who was focused on the outside world of others, things, sensory perception and action.

Extraverts tend to enjoy human interactions and thrive on being around other people. They take pleasure in activities that involve large social gatherings. An extravert is likely to find less reward in time spent alone, compared to an introvert. They are energized when around other people and are more prone to boredom when they are by themselves.

Introverts are predominantly concerned with and interested in their own mental life and are more reserved and reflective than extraverts. An introvert's physical and mental energy expands through reflection and reduces during interaction with others. They are more likely to enjoy time spent alone or in interactions with a few close friends as opposed to spending time in large groups where they are overwhelmed by the over-stimulating external environment.

Consider the differences between the extraverted professional speaker who after a presentation joins the client group for cocktails and a lively conversation and the introverted professional speaker who after the energy drain of a presentation prefers to go to his hotel room and have a few moments of quiet to regroup and regain energy.

A client may think that because a facilitator works effectively with a large group of people throughout the day or presents a stunning keynote presentation to hundreds of conference participants, the presenter would be delighted to continue to socialize following the event. This is generally true for extraverts, but usually untrue for introverts who need time away so they can recharge their energetic batteries.

If you are a mid-to-extreme *extravert*, you may find that locking yourself away to work on a writing project is not only difficult, but impossible. You need PEOPLE to discuss your ideas with, PEOPLE around you in your environment, PEOPLE interrupting you frequently before you start daydreaming about other projects, PEOPLE to take your mind off the work, and PEOPLE to reconnect you to your content.

If you have heard about authors who go away to where there is no phone, internet or contact with humans for days at a time to write, you can be certain that if they had success writing, they were introverts. Extraverts begin to get stir crazy after the first four hours, and search out the closest Starbucks within the first 24 hours to regain their social sanity. Escaping to the woods or a luxury spa is not a successful strategy for extraverts.

Compared to the extraverted author, if you are a mid-to-extreme *introvert*, you need to avoid people for longer periods of time so they won't distract you from your work and so you may concentrate on your book project. Period.

Introverts do not dislike people or try to avoid them. Even introvert Henry David Thoreau, whose famous quote, "I have never found the companion that was so companionable as solitude," scarcely spent a day totally alone, either at Walden or later at his parents' home, which was filled with boarders with whom he took great pleasure in talking. He had many friends and was entertained very frequently at the homes of Emerson and neighbors. He went walking and sailing often and was also famous for saying, "I am naturally no hermit, but might possibly sit out the sturdiest frequenter of the bar room, if my business called me thither."

Advice for Extraverts

It is very challenging for extreme extraverts to be authors – it is difficult to stand being alone by themselves for the time it takes to write something longer than a blog.

- Minimize the aloneness of writing by scheduling social time into your day so you know how long you 'still have to write' before you can take a break and communicate with another human.
- Acknowledge your Author Personality - the goal is to get the project done, not to get it done a certain way.
- Consider working in coffee shops, restaurants or libraries where there are humans around you, but not necessarily 'with' you. Pay attention to where you are the most productive: is it an upfront window seat where you see people walk by or a back table space that is quieter?
- If you choose a coffee shop as a writing or editing location, use the human noise and activity happening around you. If and when you want to engage in that noise, you can strike up a conversation with a stranger, just listen into a conversation next to you for a few minutes, or even text or call someone to join you for a coffee while you take a quick break.
- Writing is an alone activity and extreme extraverts will be easily distracted not only by other humans, but by other tasks. Set up an environment where only your current writing materials surround you. If you decide to work in your home or office, consider boxing up all other material that you won't be focusing on until after the book project is finished. Label the boxes and put them in another room, in the basement, or even in storage.

Advice for Introverts

Writing is a solitary role that introverts are more comfortable with than extraverts, yet they too can become sidetracked.

- Identify your best writing times. You may be driven to write long hours and some of those hours will be more productive than others. Pay attention to these swings in productivity and energy so you know when you are in a declining return and are better served by resting or doing other tasks.
- Be willing to tell others that when you are writing you need to be left undisturbed. If you don't live alone, this may require some tough conversations with loved ones. Identify a quiet place where you can work and consider a cheery note on your closed door, such as, "don't disturb me unless someone is bleeding or the house is on fire".
- Go away to be alone to work if you cannot find the quiet and undistracted space at home, even if it is at the library for a few serene hours.

Am I an Introvert or Extravert?

Not sure? These few questions should guide you to find an answer if you are uncertain. (To get a more in-depth understanding of your own extraverted or introverted nature, engage in a Myers-Briggs Type Indicator workshop or complete an MBTI assessment on-line.)

Are you almost never alone
or
do you like to be alone every now and then?

Do you think aloud
or
do you think first, talk later?

Do you look for inspiration from other people
or
do you look for inspiration within yourself?

Do you talk during movies, sharing your thoughts with your friend beside you
or
do you never comment during a movie?

Do you have many friends and like making new friends
or
do you have a few close friends that you will keep forever?

Do you enjoy getting phone calls from friends, even unexpectedly
or
do you get slightly annoyed when you are interrupted by a phone call?

Do you find big, crowded events energizing
or
do you find yourself exhausted by large numbers of people where there is an expectation to socialize?

Do you love to share all your news with your friends and colleagues (it doesn't seem real until you have told someone)
or
do you not need to share news to make it real and often keep it to yourself until it is big enough to 'matter'?

Do you have plans every minute of the day, moving quickly from event to event
or
do you like periods of time with no plans?

Score:
The first phrase in each question
is a more extraverted behaviour or desire.
The second phrase
Is a more introverted behaviour or desire.

4

ARE YOU PRESSURE-PROMPTED OR PLEASURE-PROMPTED

Frank was almost finished the first draft of his new book. He knew if he stayed on his plan for writing and production, his new book would be available for book signings and launch as of September 1st. He contacted three book stores and arranged signing event dates for mid-September. When he told his wife and business colleagues about his plans, they looked at him bug-eyed and questioned his sanity.

Frank told them, "If I don't book a deadline event, I won't feel pushed to finish. The embarrassment of cancelling the dates alone will drive me to completion."

Does just thinking about what Frank has done give you a heart stopping moment? The idea that an author would put those kinds of commitments out there publicly, when they can't be 100 percent certain that they will make their deadlines, might seem pretty crazy.

British philosopher Jeremy Bentham once said, "nature has placed mankind under the government of two sovereign masters: pain and pleasure. They govern us in all we do, say, and think. Every effort we make to throw off our subjection will only serve to demonstrate and confirm it."

It is a natural instinct and compulsion to seek pleasure and avoid pain. If we link more pain than pleasure to doing something, we resist doing it, or do it less consistently. If we link pleasure to an action, we will tend to do it and do it consistently.

It really isn't pain and pleasure per se that we are avoiding and desiring but the fear of pain and the anticipation of pleasure, respectively. We might think we are rational thinkers and doers, but alas our actions and procrastinations are driven by baser instincts, just as Bentham suggests.

Put yourself in Frank's shoes in the above situation and notice your emotion. If you organized a book signing for a date six months from now for a book that you're only three quarters written, how would you feel about that? Would that deadline motivate you or demotivate you? Would it make you want to go and hide under a rock, or would it make you push everything off your desk and get to it?

At each step in the Book Project Model covered in the second half of this book, you will ask yourself these two questions:

Question #1 - When I look at the individual tasks related to this step, do I feel excited or cautious?

Question #2 - Do I see myself accomplishing the tasks involved or not?

If you feel excited and see yourself moving forward towards the tasks in a particular book writing step, you probably are pleasure-prompted (motivated by the pleasure of doing and completing the tasks in this step). Your excitement will propel you forward.

If you feel ambivalent, cautious, or even nauseous about the tasks in the step ahead, you desire to avoid the pain. These emotions may manifest in procrastination and therefore you may decide you have to set up pressure that will trigger pain if you fail. In the example above, Frank has done just that – he created pressure so he will complete the steps between writing and marketing in a timely manner. He is avoiding the pain of failure through creating pressure.

If you are avoiding pain, and creating pressure so you will be prompted, or pushed to completion – you still have choices. Do you wish to garner the self-discipline to move through the tasks of this step yourself, beg or ask someone to help you with the tasks, or hire the tasks out for completion to a competent person? Determining this requires stepping back from the emotion of the possible pain ahead and making a plan that involves either using other people's skills and talents or creating a detailed strategy for completion by your sole efforts.

The challenge of girding our loins and striking up the self-discipline to attend to the tasks in any particular step is fraught with the demon procrastination. We intentionally avoid unpleasant tasks and wait for inspiration, telling ourselves we will get to it the next day. Or we justify that a particular task in the step is unnecessary, and does not need to be accomplished. Or in a few cases, we might just abandon the project and distract ourselves with other activities.

This is where understanding your Author Personality is essential. Time will drift by and the tasks will move from one 'To Do' list to the next, with the dream of a completed book remaining merely a dream and never a manifested reality.

Advice for Pressure-Prompted Authors

In Homer's Odyssey, Ulysses fought against the sirens' songs that would have led to the destruction of his ship and the death of the crew aboard.

- Avoid distractions like Ulysses' tempting sirens - whether your siren is Facebook, an invitation for coffee, an uncut lawn or a pile of unfolded laundry. Although not finishing the book isn't the death of a person, it may be the death of your dream.

Run the 12 minute race.

- Set a timer and work on the book project task for exactly 12 minutes.
- Work on an unrelated task for 12 minutes.
- Return to the unwanted book project task for another 12 minutes, and then another 12 minutes on an unrelated task.
- Continue this pattern for one hour and then reflect and plan the next segment of time.
- We can do anything for 12 minutes. Often once we get our teeth back into the task, we feel motivated to put in a longer block of time and the 12 minute race becomes unnecessary.

Chunk and order.

- Break the parts of the tasks of the step into as many smaller chunks as possible.
- Order the parts from least unpleasant to most unpleasant.
- Start the list with the most pleasant and work down to least pleasant. You may have heard the adage of starting the day with your least favorite task. This demotivating strategy works against your writing success.

Advice for Pleasure-Prompted Authors

Create a visual image of your final product.
- Create a cover for the book (even though it may change in the future) in color and place in your work area to increase your passion and motivation for the book project.
- Use it as your screensaver on your laptop, phone and other electronic tools.

Tell the story.
- Talk to others about your upcoming book and describe how you think the book will help your career or business.

5

ARE YOU A LINEAR OR A LATERAL THINKER

Georgia asked Penny to review several chapters of the book that she was writing. Penny asked for the table of contents, the chapters for review and the outlines for the remaining chapters of the book.

Georgia laughed and said, "I don't have the table of contents and won't till the book is done. I am not sure which chapter will go where. I certainly didn't do chapter outlines. I will just see where the pieces fall and it will all work out in the end."

Penny shook her head and mumbled to herself, "If this book isn't a disaster, it will be a miracle."

Georgia and Penny definitely look at this book project differently. The difference is their preference for linear (left brain) or lateral (right brain) thinking.

Have you ever sat through a personality type assessment and been told you have a brain, but only half of it is working? That the two different sides of our brain control two different modes of thinking? There is still some squabbling over the relevant science, but we have seen considerable evidence to support the idea that people do relate to information differently – one more holistically and one more logically. We can complete tasks that require lateral and linear thinking, but we have a preference for one as our dominant strategy.

Experimentation has suggested that the two different sides or hemispheres of the brain are responsible for different ways of thinking. The left is considered analytical in approach while the right is described as holistic or global. Left-brainers prefer to learn in a step-by-step or linear sequential format beginning with details leading to a conceptual understanding. Right-brainers prefer a lateral approach to learning, beginning with a general concept and then going down to specifics.

Left-brainers are associated with word meaning and logical plans, and seem to have a higher ability to recall people's names than lateral thinkers. Left-brainers are perceived as punctual, logical, sequential, rational, and objective. Right-brainers are random thinkers, and are often described as intuitive, holistic, synthesizing, subjective, impulsive, and having a talent for recalling people's faces.

Left-brain and right-brain differences also tie to what we find important in a task or project. Left-brainers are more likely to see what needs to be done, by when and how. Right-brainers are more likely to see if and why it needs to be done and who should be involved.

In the example above, Penny appears to be more left-brained and Georgia more right-brained. Penny believes that a sequential framework is necessary for pieces to fall logically into place beneath or within. Georgia does not.

Consider the metaphor of kangaroos and ladders. Penny is a ladder and Georgia a kangaroo. How would you climb a ladder? You don't start at the first rung, jump to the third, flip over to the other side of the ladder and then back to the second rung on the first side. That would be illogical, time wasting and frankly, foolish. You start at the bottom and climb to the first rung, then the second, then the third, and onwards to the top. If you are a linear thinker, your mind works exactly like a ladder, rung by rung, logically climbing in one direction, looking only at the next step in front of you.

One of the consequences of being an author who is a ladder, or linear thinker, is that if you get stuck on a chapter, you might not finish your book project. If you think you have to write chapter two before chapter three, your thinking preference may paralyze you from moving forward to success.

Do you remember the days of grade school book reports? One day, your teacher announced the book report assignment with instructions to first write a table of contents. Did you think, "That's logical," and then went forth and wrote a table of contents, followed by a chapter for each of those items under that table of contents, in linear order - chapter 1, 2, 3, 4, 5. If this sounds like you, you are probably a linear thinker.

However, if you were uncertain as to what content should be used where, the instructions from your teacher were frustrating and difficult to complete. To succeed, you may have needed to work on many sections simultaneously and in the end make it all line up and make sense, rather than address the assignment in a step-by-step process. Lateral thinkers – kangaroos - do not climb ladders in their minds. They are more likely to jump about quickly from place to place and eventually arrive in the desired location. Kangaroos have to write the whole report and then go back and write the table of contents.

In conclusion, the two major differences of lateral/linear thinking that affect Author Personality are:

1. The left side of the brain processes information in a linear manner. It processes from part to whole. It takes pieces, lines them up, and arranges them in a logical order; then it draws conclusions. The right brain, however, processes from whole to parts, holistically. It starts with the answer. It sees the big picture first, not the details. A left-brainer outlines the book and then writes it, a right brainer writes the book and then outlines it.

2. Left-brainers process in sequence. They are list makers and enjoy making master schedules and daily plans. They complete tasks in order and take pleasure in checking them off when they are accomplished. The right brain, however, is random. A right-brainer moves from task to task and back again, and is often seen as being unorganized by others working on the same project. A right-brainer may write a book, fifteen chapters all at one time. A left-brainer is most comfortable writing one chapter at a time, in order.

Am I a Linear or Lateral Thinker?

If you are still struggling with understanding how this difference affects your Author Personality, try this exercise:

1. Tape a flipchart piece of paper to a wall

2. Write the name of the book/or book theme in the middle of the page.

3. Step back and close your eyes.

4. Think about the content of the book.

5. Open your eyes and step forward.

6. As quickly as you can put one word or two word phrases on the flipchart to describe the pieces of content.

7. Step away from the flipchart.

8. Go to page 40.

9. Does your flipchart page look like example A or example B?

A

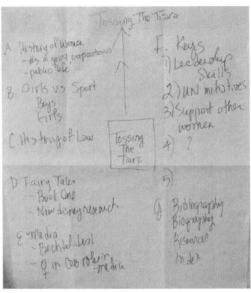

B

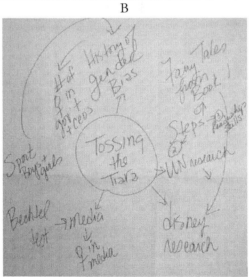

Diagram A is the mind map (lateral content dump) of my new book, *Tossing the Tiara – Keys to Creating Powerful Women Leaders*. Due to my lateral way of thinking, I had to force myself to construct a linear content outline which appears in Diagram B.

6

ARE YOU AN EARLY BIRD OR A NIGHT OWL

John reached over and released the buzzer of his alarm clock and then relaxed back into the warm covers of his bed and groaned. It was 5 a.m. and he was determined to get an early start on his new book project. He had heard from several book gurus that if he wished to be a successful author, he should get up early and attack the book first thing before he was sucked into the regular schedule of his day. This was day four of the plan, but the only thing John had managed to do was fall asleep over his computer while he was waiting for inspiration to strike. If this was how to become a best-selling author, he was in trouble.

John's problem is not that he isn't motivated to write his book. His problem is that he isn't respecting his own Author Personality.

Benjamin Franklin was famous for his phrase, "Early to bed and early to rise will make a man healthy, wealthy and wise." But that was assuming that the man who goes to bed early can drop off to sleep and the man who rises early will have the physical and mental acuity to take charge of his day.

Carolyn Schur, author of *Birds of a Different Feather: Early Birds and Night Owls Talk About Their Characteristic Behaviours*, believes that up to 25% of us are night owls, with approximately 15% of us being early birds and 60% of us being Intermediates. (Intermediates favor a bedtime between 11 p.m. and midnight and wake time between 7 and 8 a.m.)

Many people believe that this circadian rhythm or time preference is something a person could change if they wanted to. But trying to become an early bird when you are a night owl is like writing with your right hand when you are left handed. Just like writing with your less dominant hand, working on creative projects in your non-peak hours leads to lower productivity and minimized creativity.

Whether our body is an early bird, night owl or intermediate is determined by our internal master clock. Our circadian clock addresses sleep and wakefulness, body temperature and metabolic rate. When we wake up in the morning at our natural time (not by alarm clock), that waking is triggered by a rise in our body temperature. Alternatively, our sleep hormones and sleepiness is triggered by a low in our body temperature in the evening. The time your natural body alarms go off determine your circadian identity and whether you will be an early bird (who loves to leap out of bed at 6 a.m. with vim and vigor) or a night owl (who loves stay to in bed until noon and then work into the wee hours).

John would be better served to work later into the evening on his book. His attempts to rise early and be productive are at odds with his body that is determined to become only truly alert and creative later in the day.

Are you a Night Owl or an Early Bird?

Choose one phrase in each set:

In the morning . . . .

    A. I don't usually rely on an alarm clock or I wake and get out of bed as soon as the alarm rings.
    B. I hit the snooze button. I hit the snooze button. I hit the snooze button. Eventually, I drag myself out of bed.

At 9:30 in the evening . . . .

    A. I have been in bed for an hour.
    B. I am doing the laundry, cleaning the garage, working on paperwork ...

The time of day that I am most alert and energetic is . . .
    A. Early morning
    B. Afternoon
    C. Late evening.

If you are a night owl, your choices were b, b, c and if you are an early bird, your choices were a, a, a.

You may be an intermediate, if you found yourself saying, "Well, sometimes, I do this and sometimes, I do that. It just depends." Or if you chose some early bird responses and some night owl responses.

Intermediates can be more flexible with their schedules, sometimes adhering to early bird schedules and sometimes to night owl schedules as the need arises. They are, however, much more affected by the "post lunch dip," that very strong desire for sleep in the early afternoon.

The above quiz is used with permission from its author: Carolyn Schur.

7

THE MILKING STOOL OF YOUR BOOK AND BUSINESS

Twenty years ago, I was fortunate to be involved with a group of Canadian women entrepreneurs who created a non-profit organization called Women Entrepreneurs of Saskatchewan (WES). Funded by membership fees and government grants, our goal was to remove the barriers to success for women entrepreneurs. As President in the early years, I had the privilege of meeting hundreds of business women and hearing their stories and dreams about being in their own business.

What I found over and again was that when a business struggled, the problem was not that the entrepreneur was ineffective in the production of her service or product. Rather, the business failed if the entrepreneur was not as good at running the front end (marketing and vision) or back end (accounting and administration) of her enterprise. The more I studied small business as the leader of WES, I began to see business as a future, present, and past continuum with specific tasks and roles at each stop on the continuum. Today I realize that the same principles that apply to successful small businesses applies to book projects as well.

In his book, *The E-Myth*, Michael E. Gerber described why business owners fail. He suggested that there were three competency areas we need to master to be successful in business: marketing, technical and financial. For example, if I owned a restaurant, the technical skills involved would be cooking, serving and clearing. The required marketing skills would be designing and fulfilling marketing plans and strategies to get patrons to come to the restaurant and continue to return. The third component, the financial skills, would involve inventory control, sales taxes, payroll, bank deposits, and year end audits.

In his book, *How to Start a Business and Ignite Your Life*, Ernesto Sirolli describes these three elements as the entrepreneur, the product person, and the financial manager. In this model, the person who creates the product or delivers the service is called the product person. They are the doers whose sweat and tears facilitate innovation and creation. Smart product people recognize that success in a business project does not rest solely on their shoulders or efforts, but also on the efforts of effective marketing and prudent financial decision making and execution.

In the book world, a traditional (or legacy) publisher would take the financial management and some of the marketing off the shoulders of the author. The author could then focus his talents and passion on the creation of the product – the book. He is the technician.

Writers who have worked with traditional publishers (where the author receives an advance payment against their percentage of future book revenue and is not requested or required to contribute financially to the project) recognize that although the financial decisions may be removed from the author's control and responsibility, it is the author who is partly and sometimes primarily responsible for book sales. The technician has become the entrepreneur as well, to use Sirolli's terms.

In my home, I have a brown, three legged stool that was once a working chair in my husband's grandfather's dairy farm in Ontario.

This stool serves as a wonderful metaphor for the three core roles of building a successful business or launching a successful self-published book.

Let's look deeper to see why this three legged stool is so important to your success as an author and how your Author Personality (the four questions) and the Book Project Model (obsess through to reposition) must be seen in concert with the three roles of the milking stool: the Marketer/Entrepreneur (ME), the Writer/Author (WA) and the Manager/Administrator (MA).

The ME is focused on the future sales of book and the related services, the WA is focused on the here and now of getting the book written, and the MA is focused on making sure you make money on your past efforts.

By creating a triangular frame through which each of the Author Personality questions are asked, an author can clearly see what roles need to be filled at each stage of the Book Project Model and which of those related tasks should be completed by him or by others.

Marketer/Entrepreneur or ME

This role may begin the day you have your first author seizure. That moment when a light bulb goes on inside your head and you dream the dream of being a published author.

The ME decides what is the vision for the book, the mini-mission of the project inside the larger mission of your career or business. The ME is the grand strategist, the creator of something new that will saturate an existing or create a new market, tap into future trends and embrace the unknown. Sounds inspiring, doesn't it? The ME is all about creating possibilities which the WA and MA will need to manifest.

Manager/Administrator or MA

The MA is pragmatic and if this role is left unfilled or ignored, there will be no order or predictability. The MA is the part of us that goes to Staples and buys bankers boxes, takes them back to the office and systematically stores all the various papers in alpha-numeric, color coded hanging file folders.

A ME lives in the future and a MA lives in the past; the ME craving control over the future and the MA craving control over the past. A ME is all about change and a MA clings to the status quo. This creates tension between the vision of the ME and the pragmatic drive for completion and order of the MA.

Writer/Author or WA

The Writer/Author is the one who has the expertise and puts high value on the content of the book. He might believe in his ideas so much that he deludes himself into thinking that if he only writes the book, the marketing and management will take care of itself. If the book is good enough, it will sell itself. Or the author is focused on being published as the end result and having his words in print is the true satisfaction. He will just write the book and see how it goes.

Balance

Without balance between all three legs of the milking stool, the tyranny of one dominant role might control the project and risk failure or low success. A book that doesn't sell, a book without a vision, 6000 books in your basement, an unwritten book, or books that are sold for less than they cost to produce are all possible outcomes to an unbalanced book project. All three roles (ME, MA and WA) must be given opportunity, freedom and nourishment or your book project (as with any business) will be lopsided and unstable.

A ME heavy business, without a strong MA to give order or a WA to put the strategy to work, will suffer a dramatic and early death.

A Manager/Administrator driven project would produce boxes of research carefully filed away, and, no doubt, color coded. But there is no need for the boxes of research notes, if no book is being written.

A Writer/Author driven book project without the Marketer/Entrepreneur's vision and Manager/Administrator's supervision to keep to task could result in a Writer/Author who works till he drops, but not necessarily on the path of a marketable or profitable book.

Remember, you do not have to personally complete all the tasks required by the roles of the MA, ME and even WA. But they still have to be done. This is where we partner with others, beg friends and colleagues to assist, or hire others to help.

8

LEGACY PUBLISHING, ASSSISTED-PUBLISHING, OR SELF-PUBLISHING: AUTHOR CHOICE?

Although we think of self-publishing as a new concept, Twain and authors before him found ingenious ways of realizing their ideas in print other than through a traditional or legacy publisher. From serialized book segments published in newspapers and magazines to printing his own books and flogging them himself, Twain was an entrepreneur, an author and a great manager of his own creative output.

This chapter and the next chapter following will help you understand the three ways of publishing your words of wisdom so you as the author can make the logical choice for your book project.

A traditional or **legacy publisher** is a pre-digital era publishing company.

Its role in the book industry is to:

- select book projects
- assume the financial risk of development, production, marketing and sales
- provide editorial support
- deliver the content in a consumable form (both printed format and electronic)
- release the book into the world of buyers and reviewers so that it will be found and purchased
- publicize and market the book to build awareness and demand among book stores and other distribution networks
- take orders from bookstores and other buyers
- produce the books or files and warehouse physical books
- deliver the product to the buyers
- collect the money owed
- pay the author a small amount of said collected money (also known as a royalty or percentage of sales).

In the **self-publishing** model, today's author performs a similar list of tasks, often with the difference being that the self-publisher does not warehouse books but uses a print on demand service to produce just-in-time amounts of product. There is no advance given to the author, but neither is there a publisher package fee as with assisted-publishing.

I consider the phrase **'assisted publishing'** an appropriate one. Like the in-between assisted-living residences of senior citizens who have foregone living independently but are not ready for a nursing home, so too can authors hover in an in-between place between legacy publishing and self-publishing. This type of publishing arrangement is where a publishing services agency provides some of the above services of the traditional publisher for a fee to the author, but also leaves more decision making to the author as well.

In the following pages, we will discuss the pros and cons of each publishing method.

Pros and Cons of Legacy Publishing

Do any of these publishers sound familiar?

Putnam - Ballantine - Dell - Bantam - Random House - Potter Portfolio- Puffin – Tundra - Signal - Allen Lane – Emblem Anchor – Vintage Appetite – Penguin – Viking – Knopf – Bond Street - Doubleday – Hamish Hamilton McClelland & Stewart

We have seen them on the inside front pages of books we read and on the spines of the books we browse in bookstores. We may secretly dream of our name being on their list of authors. What you might not know is that the list above is all one company: Penguin Random House.

Although they may use the term *publisher* or *publishing company*, all the names above are actually imprints of the newly amalgamated publisher Penguin Random House (PRH) which now controls one third of the Canadian legacy printing industry. Sister companies in countries throughout the world hold similar control over their domestic publishing industries.

In January 2012, just prior to the Penguin and Random House merger announcement, Random House took control of McClelland & Stewart and its children's book imprint, Tundra.

The new organization held by German firm Bertelsmann (53%) and British firm Pearson (47%) is headquartered in New York City and operates in 20 countries and in five continents. The imprints listed above are only a few of their 250 global imprints. Penguin Random House publishes 70,000 digital and 15,000 print titles annually.

What does this mean for you and other authors?

This creates a near-monopoly that will be able to dictate financial terms to authors who now face fewer and fewer places to traditionally publish their work. Although legacy publishers profess to providing choice between imprints, the author's ability to negotiate has become more limited.

In a spring 2015 article in the Globe and Mail, Kristin Cochrane (President & Publisher, Random House of Canada) said that there will still be competition and that Penguin Random House "owe authors' representatives choice" between imprints. Yet, Lynn Henry, Knopf Canada's publishing director said, "We don't really compete so much financially as we do in terms of the vision. And often our publishing visions can be very different."

Even Brad Martin (President and CEO of Penguin Random House Canada) stated, "Why would you bid against each other? Scale is supposed to mean something." He further admitted that there will be fewer books published under the joint operation of Penguin Random House than under the two separate entities of Penguin and Random House combined. What some agents and authors see as a devastating occurrence, Penguin Random House sees as good business.

So for the author, legacy publishing isn't a closed door, but the doorway is definitely getting narrower.

Why are authors attracted to legacy publishers?

It is true that the usual reasons (validation by the industry, credibility, social proof, and prestige) are declining in significance as books created through self-publishing and assisted-publishing increase in reader market share, particularly in the eBook market.

What the legacy publishers *do* give you as an author is top quality distribution and print production, and assistance from a professional team of designers, editors and publicists. They also take away the economic concerns of production expenses and frequently provide an advance payment against future sales.

What are the drawbacks to legacy publishing?

Many authors believe that once they have signed a contract with a book publisher, they only need to complete the book on deadline to manifest success. However, authors need to consider the drawbacks of traditional publishing in the areas of income and control. The publishing house generally controls title, cover design, back cover design regarding author biography, interior design, date of release, testimonials or advance praise of the book, book price, and promotion and marketing plans.

The amount of time between when the initial contract is signed and the date the publisher releases the book to the world could be years. If your book release date affects your other career or business initiatives, this delay could be frustrating and troublesome. The more time sensitive your book's content, the more concerned you should be regarding timeframe.

Advances and royalties are two words every author likes to hear. An advance is where a publisher advances the author a sum of money so the author can finish the writing of the book or complete the necessary work to take the book from first draft through editing to publication. Royalties are a percentage of book sales which the author receives from the publisher. The royalties are not paid until the advance has been absorbed. For example, if I received a $10,000 advance from the publisher and negotiated a royalty of 10% on a sticker price of $20.00, 5000 books would need to be sold before I received my first royalty check.

Unfortunately if this is your first book, unless you recently lost the United States election for vice president, spent months in a space station or shot a global terrorist, your advance against royalties may be miniscule. The upside is that if your book sells well, there is a smaller advance to absorb before the royalties on the book start to be paid. Some authors never sell beyond their advance. Royalty rates depend on the publishing house and a 7-10% royalty is average.

Every book needs a marketing and promotion plan. Depending on the value of the book to the publisher, the author will be given limited publicity and marketing investment. Unless you are one of the earlier mentioned celebrities, expect to be organizing signings and media appearances for your first book on your own.

Pros and Cons to Assisted-Publishing

The ad screams, "Do you want to be a published author? We can help your dream come true!"

The first step for many authors was responding to an email or advertisement from IUniverse, Balboa Press, HayHouse or another assisted-publishing agency. The dream of authorship floats before the aspiring author's eyes, tempting the author into the dream of best-selling stardom.

All assisted-publishing agencies are not the same. This in-between zone of full control and responsibility over your self-published project and almost absolute surrender of working with a traditional publisher has many shades of grey.

Because the author and publisher are in a financial partnership of sorts, gaining agreement for your book to be accepted is startlingly easy. The author is, in some ways, hiring out the work of: cover and internal design, editorial support, production of print, formatting of eBooks, distribution to bookstores and other buyers, delivery of the product to the buyers, and accounts receivable. It all depends upon how much the author wants to spend. Some agencies even provide the service of ghost writing your book where you supply the content (interviews, previous writings, audio and video) and the ghost writes the book, with you remaining the 'author'.

Unlike traditional publishing, the author pays up front for a publishing package selected from a menu of services. For authors who have little understanding of the book marketplace, this may be a good place to start with your first book.

The secret to using assisted-publishing agencies is to be clear regarding exactly what you are purchasing and what the quality of those services will be. Remember that you are buying a series of services. Do not be so flattered that you are remiss in checking out agencies thoroughly. If this is your publishing choice, ask colleagues about their experiences, review the agency's reputation through social media, and ask the agency for references.

Pros and Cons of Self-Publishing

Authors are attracted to self-publishing over traditional and assisted-publishing for three reasons:

- The author retains more revenue from book sales
- The author controls all aspects of design and content
- The author determines pricing and timelines for production.

The image of self-publishing over the past decade has shifted from one of a 'vanity press' where authors paid for the printing of their books (some well written and designed, many not so much) to one of a logical and respected business practice.

The usual motivations for pursuing traditional publishing are declining as readers are increasingly purchasing self-published books in print and by eBook. It is a brave new world for the author who chooses to learn about the self-publishing industry. A self-published author doesn't need to master all the elements of the book industry, but she should know the basics so she can decide what tasks and processes she should do herself and what she should hire out, beg a friend to complete, or partner with others to get done.

If a first-time author thinks that the tasks of self-publishing are overwhelming and that a publishing contract with a traditional publisher would guarantee all those troubling elements would be handled by others, the author may spend years pursing a contract instead of seeing their words in print.

9
THE BOOK PROJECT MODEL: OBSESS TO REPOSITION

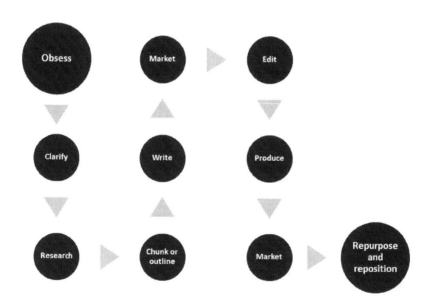

When we write, we may recognize the steps: research, write, produce, and sell. However, the path is a bit more complex than that if we wish to become a successful author as painlessly as possible.

Welcome to the Book Project Model. It includes ten steps: obsess, clarify, research, chunk or outline, write, market, edit, produce, market, repurpose and reposition.

At each of these steps, we reflect on the Author Personality questions and the three roles of the Milking Stool.

10
STEP ONE OBSESS

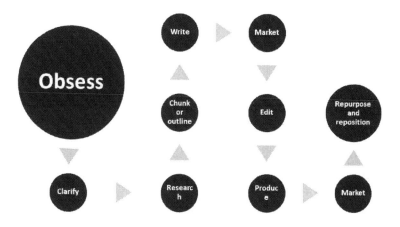

What is motivating you to write this book? The top four reasons I have found that motivate authors to write non-fiction books are: to increase credibility, to produce a product for a revenue stream, to codify knowledge and finally because the idea keeps the author up at night and is calling out to be put into a book.

For you, it could be a combination of a few or even all four. If you do not have a compelling reason to motivate you to write, chances are your dream of authorship will be an unfulfilled wish.

Credibility

A published work in an area of our expertise increases our professional credibility. Certainly years of experience and several letters following our name are useful, but how do we distinguish ourselves from others who also have several years of experience and several letters following their names? A book in our area of expertise, especially with information and examples tied to our clients' industry, geography and demographic reality sets us apart.

When a prospective client challenges my consulting or speaking fee (with the usual line about having a low budget), I have an appropriate response. I speak in the area of leading diverse workforces and if the contract is for a presentation on generational differences, I can bring to the buyer's attention that with my book *Generation Y and the New Work Ethic*, I am one of only a handful of authors on this topic with Canadian content and statistics. I am not just another presenter on the generational topic; I might be *the* speaker on the topic.

You rarely get questioned about your fee when you are the expert. Having the credibility of not only being an author, but also an author on the subject that the client is struggling with, compels a client to hire you over another person speaking or consulting on your subject.

If your book is driven by a credibility motive, ask yourself: "How will this book help me continue to get my full fee, or an increased fee, if I am a speaker? How will this help me to be the one they choose, if I am a consultant or coach? How will this book attract more business?"

Revenue

Choosing to produce a book as an additional revenue source can be a good idea, but is dependent upon the author's ability to market and sell the book. A strong distribution network, presentations and other event exposure, effective social media strategies, and a strong acuity to the on-line market all help to achieve sales.

For speaker and trainers, we are fortunate that we have built-in distribution for our products to some degree. We can sell products at the back of the room of our presentations and include books as part of the contract with our clients.

Revenue is easier to achieve in a quicker time frame. When I published my first book, *Lies and Fairy Tales that Deny Women Happiness*, I needed to purchase 5000 copies to make the book cost effective. To make my last book, *Generation Y and the New Work Ethic*, cost effective, I only needed to purchase 400 copies. Thanks to just-in-time printing, we are long past the days of having thousands of unsold books in our basements or garages. Thanks to CreateSpace (Amazon's book publishing arm), we can produce 50 copies as price effectively as 5000 copies ten years ago.

Obsession

Do your ideas keep you up at night? That is why I wrote my first book. I simply could not quit thinking about it. Now that might be true for me and never true for you. But if you are thinking about an idea that is more than just a keynote speech, start thinking about it in context to a book.

Codify Ponderings

Codifying your ponderings into a book may make you a better consultant and speaker in a couple of ways:

Do you remember the infamous north-eastern American university study where a certain number of students wrote down their goals for the future, and the rest of the class did not? In the study, the few who wrote down their goals ended up making more money than the rest of the class all together. Sounds fantastic, but alas, it was bogus. I cannot count how many times I have heard that same phantom research repeated. Codifying our thoughts into a document that will become public pushes us to prove the things that we profess.

Professional Innovation Catalyst, Toni Newman suggests that we should continuously be creating innovative value, demonstrating innovative value and delivering innovative value. She challenged me to evaluate to what degree I am researching and creating 'new code' that is provocative, unique, mine alone, and absolutely true.

Codifying our ponderings forces the development of new code which then ripples back out in our keynotes, coaching, speaking, workshops and consulting.

Step One: Obsess
Through the Author Personality

1. introvert or extravert?
2. pressure-prompted or pleasure-prompted?
3. linear or lateral thinker?
4. early bird or night owl?

Does your Author Personality affect how you approach Step One: Obsess? If so, how?

_____
_____
_____
_____

Balancing the Milking Stool Roles

- Marketer/Entrepreneur or ME
- Manager/Administrator or MA
- Writer/Author or WA

Consider the publishing tasks that are listed at the beginning of Chapter 8. Which tasks of each role do you wish to take on in this step? Which tasks of this step should you partner with others, ask for help or hire out?

_____
_____
_____
_____

11
STEP TWO CLARIFY

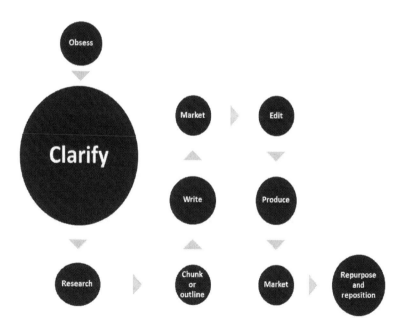

In the Obsess step, we determined why we want to write the book. In the Clarify step, the author must answer the following five questions related to the book's structure and reading audience:

Question #1
How do you want your readers to be enlightened, entertained and educated?

Question #2
What is the geographic location of your readers?

Question #3
What is the theme and title of your book?

Question #4
What will the book include and what will the book exclude?

Question #5
What is the book structure - what kind of book is it?

Question #1 - How do you want your readers to be enlightened, entertained and educated?

Every book has a combination of these three elements. In my first bestselling book, *War and Peace in the Workplace*, the emphasis was on education, with a lighter focus on enlightenment and just a smidge of entertainment. You might not think that a book that addresses gender differences, First Nations treaty rights, and the history of immigration is one that lends itself to entertainment. However, regardless of the subject matter, entertaining stories or facts can lighten the load of the educational goal of a book.

On the flipside, my first fiction book, *If It Wasn't for the Money*, had an obvious emphasis on entertainment. But it also had a smidge of education regarding domestic violence and a bit of enlightenment regarding the corruption in the junior mining industry.

Not only is there the decision to be made as to the balance of entertainment, education and enlightenment in the book, you must also determine: what exactly do you want the readers to find entertaining, what lessons do you want the readers to learn, and what 'hmmm' or 'aha' moments do you wish your readers to experience?

Question #2 - What is the geographic location of your readers?

Are you perplexed by this question? Was the first answer that came to your mind – the entire world?

Certainly with the magic of Amazon, Kindle, NOOK and Kobo, your books can reach the far corners of the planet, but the question is - where do your ideal readers live and who are you writing the book for? Who is your target reader? By determining the location of your audience's geography, you determine the scope of your research and the tone of your writing.

For example, my book, *War and Peace in the Workplace*, is based on Canadian statistics. I have readers who asked if I was planning on writing an American edition. I had questions from fellow authors as to the wisdom of not focusing on American issues with the US book market being so much larger than the Canadian one. My book, *Generation Y and the New Work Ethic*, is based on Canadian statistics with a heavier weight placed on western Canadian stories. Western Canada is the geographic location of business owners, leaders and managers that are the target audience for both that book and diversity speaking business.

I do not always write for a Canadian market. This book on Author Personality, for example, is targeted to speakers, trainers and other experts who wish to write a non-fiction book. This is a smaller audience spread further geographically. I need to market to Canadian, American and European readers and therefore I use references that allow them to see themselves reflected in my writing. That is why I am using American English instead of Canadian English (color over colour) or British English (organization over organisation).

You may be an American speaker who thinks that he speaks all over the United States. But do you really? Do you speak primarily in the South West or the North East, or in three major cities? Would it serve you to target your book more specifically to an area, using stories and anecdotes from there? Would regional references make the book more powerful?

Question #3 - What is the theme and title of the book?

Think of your book theme or title as your North Star. It keeps you on track through the writing and editing and if you are pleasure-prompted, it will inspire you to finish. Like the cover, your title will draw you to complete the project.

Consider the influence of a book title on the Author Personality question of lateral or linear thinking. If you are a lateral thinker, you will be drawn to a metaphorical or graphic title. If you are a linear thinker, you will more likely to be drawn to a linear title.

However, a good title addresses both linear and lateral readers and has a graphic/metaphorical major title followed by a linear descriptive subtitle. For example, one of my newer books due out fall 2015, is called *Tossing the Tiara – The Key to Creating Powerful Women Leaders*. 'Tossing the Tiara' is the lateral title. 'The Key to Creating Powerful Women Leaders' is the linear title.

Consider these descriptive (linear) titles:

1. *The Story of Success*
2. *Esoteric Math and Astrological Techniques for the Market Trader*
3. *Leadership for the 21st Century*
4. *How to Profit from the Coming Demographic Shift*
5. *The Battle Over the Future of Food and Farming in America*

Rather dull, aren't they? Yet they are all best-sellers. All six titles are the subtitle (linear half) of the full title of the book.

Readers, especially lateral thinkers, are drawn to the graphic/metaphorical part of the title. Here are the titles again, including their preceding lateral main titles and authors:

1. *Outliers - The Story of Success* (Malcolm Gladwell)
2. *The Lost Science - Esoteric Math and Astrological Techniques for the Market Trader* (Malcolm Bucholtz)
3. *Escape from Oz - Leadership for the 21st Century* (Jeanne Martinson)
4. *Boom Bust & Echo - How to Profit from the Coming Demographic Shift* (David K. Foot)
5. *Foodopoly - The Battle Over the Future of Food and Farming in America* (Wenonah Hauter)

Question #4 - What will the book include and what will the book exclude?

You cannot cover all the issues related to the topic of your book any more than you could cover all your ideas in a half-day workshop or a ninety minute keynote presentation. Don't try to. This is why understanding first how you want your audience to be changed by your book is so essential.

For example, this book is focused on the author who is self-publishing or is using an assisted-publishing agency to complete their book project. Therefore *Hemingway or Twain?* excludes information about obtaining an agent, finding a publisher, and writing book proposals. The book is focused on the Author Personality and not the finer details of the production and marketing elements. Therefore it excludes information on the different kinds of direct to print systems and complex social media marketing strategies, but includes how production and marketing are impacted by the Author Personality.

Question #5 - What is the book structure, what kind of book is it?

Are you a book snob? Do you think there is a 'best' kind of book? Is a biography better than a cookbook? A literary novel better than a mystery? A business book better than a how-to book? What is the best kind of book to write? Is one kind of book better than another?

Malcolm Gladwell puts that question to rest. When asked what kind of literature he enjoys, he replied, spy novels and confessed that he has by conservative estimate - several hundred novels with the word 'spy' in the title.

The author's job is to write a book that someone else finds useful enough to dish out the cash to match the sticker price. Whether it is a self-help, how to, academic, business, or biography – no genre has more or less value.

The most common types of non-fiction would include: compilations, biography, autobiography or memoir, how to, business, issue oriented, and self-help.

Compilations

Creating a book in conjunction with several other authors seems to some people an easy way to get a book together. In theory, you only have to write a chapter or two. However, it might be more difficult than you think if you wish to have a book that is cohesive, stress-free and published on time.

I am in the process of writing a book with 15 women in their 80s, 90s and 100s. The book, titled *Nurses of Wintergreene,* began as a tribute to my mother, a retired nurse. I realized that only our family would be interested in my mother's story, but the stories of a collection of nurses who trained in the post-Nightingale and pre-university era would be an interesting book and marketable through several avenues. That said, it has been a challenge to schedule interviews with the retired nurses around my travel schedule and their doctor's appointments and months away visiting relatives.

In 2012, I wrote a chapter for an academic book titled *Leading in Complex Worlds*. It seemed like an easy enough task to transfer my graduate school thesis on comparing corporate and criminal leaders into a chapter. Five editors and a year later, the finished book was a compilation of 2011's top academic research according to the International Leadership Association. Yet the chapters seem unrelated and without a master message. Outside of academia, this book is unsellable.

Biography

Is there someone you admire whose story must be told? Are they newsworthy? Is their story unique? Uplifting? Outrageous? An example might be the biography of Florence Bean James (*Fists upon a Star: A Memoir of Love, Theatre, and Escape from McCarthyism*) written by Jean Freeman. James was a pioneering American theatre director, whose devastating experience with McCarthyism led her to eventually flee to Canada. Born in 1892, she was a suffragette in New York City and was the first director to put Jimmy Cagney on stage. That is the kind of fascinating character that warrants a biography.

Autobiography or Memoir

Are you fascinating? Uplifting? Outrageous? Are you a medical marvel? Or an astronaut? Perhaps you led a country at one time? If not, your autobiography will only be bought by your mother.

How to Books

Do you have a talent, skill or process you wish to share? Consider these actual book titles:
- How to Build a Robot
- How to Make Money Blogging
- Ten Steps to Building an Adobe House

Business

Many non-fiction books are business books. Some are written by CEOs of Fortune 500 companies who want to share their knowledge. Some are written by people like you and me who have knowledge they wish to share to a larger audience.

Issue Oriented or Self-Help

Issue oriented books, whether they delve into politics, social issues, or environmental awareness, both inform and have a call to action for the reader. For example, my book, *Lies and Fairy Tales that Deny Women Happiness,* explored how fairy tales shape the belief systems of young women. It is also a self-help book that I hope young women will read and be encouraged by to make better career and relationship decisions.

Pure self-help are often related to an area of physical health or mental wellness.

The five questions asked in this chapter must be answered before you start the book (or at least answered to the best of your ability at the time). Once you are immersed in a book project, it becomes an unwieldy beast. Half way down the track, it is a difficult train to turn. This is why sometimes authors get partly through a project, realize it is not going in the direction they thought or want and they toss the unfinished manuscript in a drawer.

It is also useful to go back and revisit these answers at each step in the Book Project Model to ensure that the answers are still valid and that you are on the write (pun intended) track.

Advice for Asking Others for Input

As you ponder the answers to the five questions discussed in this chapter, bounce your ideas off others and get input. Consider:

- Choose a focus group of two or three people (or more if you are an extravert), explain the reason for writing the book and ask them each of the five questions.
- If you are an introvert, journal your thoughts on the five questions so you are prepared to chat to friends and colleagues.
- Post your book idea and questions on your Facebook page and ask for feedback. If appropriate post it in your Facebook and LinkedIn groups for input. (Only ask one question at a time or the threads may become confusing).
- If you are an extravert, bring up the topic of your new book whenever the opportunity arises and pay attention to the feedback. Jot down any good ideas as soon as you can before you forget the input.
- Have one-on-one conversations with those who would be buyers of your book. If you see your clients as typical buyers of the book, ask them what they'd like to see in it. What are the key questions they have on the subject of interest? What are their hot buttons? What is keeping them up at night in regards to the subject?
- Include lateral and linear thinkers in your conversations.
- If you are asking for feedback, respect the night owl/early bird preference of those who you are asking for creative input. What would be the best time for them to think about the topic or attend a focus group?

Step Two: Clarify
Through the Author Personality

1. introvert or extravert?
2. pressure-prompted or pleasure-prompted?
3. linear or lateral thinker?
4. early bird or night owl?

Does your Author Personality affect how you approach Step Two: Clarify? If so, how?

_____
_____
_____
_____

Balancing the Milking Stool Roles

- Marketer/Entrepreneur or ME
- Manager/Administrator or MA
- Writer/Author or WA

Consider the publishing tasks that are listed at the beginning of Chapter 8. Which tasks of each role do you wish to take on in this step? Which tasks of this step should you partner with others, ask for help or hire out?

_____
_____
_____
_____

12
STEP THREE
RESEARCH

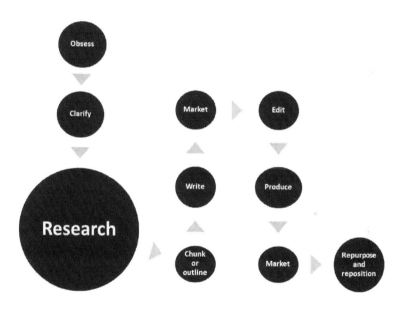

Are you an APE or a PEA? A PEA (print, eBook, audio) creates a printed book, then creates an eBook and then perhaps an audio book. An APE (audio, print, eBook) takes all of her recorded presentations on audio, sends them off to **www.fiverr.com** or **www.esource.com**

to have it transcribed into a document, adds additional stories or pieces of research, creates a final printed book and then an eBook.

Do you think you are an APE or a PEA? Not sure if you are a vegetable or animal, uncertain as to which writing style might suit you best?

The APE route sounds easier, but an author might find herself frustrated if the flow of the book is not the same flow as the recordings. Neither is wrong or right. It is a matter of recognizing the diversity of your preference and making the choice that works best for you.

How do we research? Where does the information come from?

In this book's Introduction, we discussed the value of your current and previous presentations, workshops and writings. You no doubt have a great deal of material already, so there is no need to reinvent the wheel.

The key is to first evaluate your current content for relevance and accuracy. Secondly, determine the areas in which you wish to dig deeper. Thirdly, pursue the research that will develop the book that speaks to your theme and adds value for your reader. Ask yourself: what research exists on your topic that you have not previously pursued? I know this, but how do I know it? What is this 'knowing' based on?

Consider these sources: interviews with other experts, academic sources, your clients' stories, and your own experiences.

Interviews with other experts

We don't need to know everything about every element of our research. We only need to know someone who does have that expertise, interview them and then cite them appropriately. For example, when I was writing the section on work ethic in my generational differences book, I was stumbling over how the term 'work ethic' is defined. I interviewed an expert in the field of ethics, Joe Sherren. As both a business consultant and university lecturer, Joe's qualifications provided excellent balance for a book targeted at a business market.

If you interview an expert for your book, ensure that you give them a preview of the content to ensure you referenced them correctly. Malcolm Gladwell, author of the books: *Tipping Point, Blink, Outliers,* and *David and Goliath* cautions, "My rule is that if I interview someone, they should never read what I have to say about them and regret having given me the interview."

Academic sources

Be careful as to where you source 'academic' research. Pollsters, media and well intentioned scientists have done much to create misinformation resulting in error at the hands of authors. Consider these examples:

Do you believe that blondes have more fun? Dr. Katherine M.H. Blackford wrote books in the 1920s on the workplace and said, "In brief, always and everywhere, the normal blonde has positive, dynamic, driving, aggressive, domineering, impatient, active, quick, hopeful, speculative, changeable and variety-loving characteristics; while the normal brunette has negative, static, conservative, imitative, submissive, cautious, painstaking, patient, plodding, slow, deliberate, serious, thoughtful, specializing characteristics."

A subsequent study done by Donald G. Paterson and Katherine E. Ludgate at the University of Minnesota, using 94 judges and 374 blonde and brunette interview subjects discovered the following:

1. Brunettes were found to possess blonde traits to the same extent that blondes do.
2. Blondes were found to possess brunette traits to the same extent that brunettes do.

The study, carried out in 1922 and published in the *Journal of Personnel Research* under the title "Blonde and Brunette Traits: A Quantitative Study" indicates that blondes and brunettes do not have distinctive characteristics, yet many people still believe blondes have more fun. It is commonly believed blondes are more positive, dynamic, and changeable - while brunettes are deliberate, thoughtful and conservative.

Some writers or researchers, such as Blackford above are just plain wrong. Yet their opinions are repeated and can even create societal beliefs.

Although as authors we wish to simplify concepts and make sense of complex research, we must look deeper than media sound bites and ask tough questions. In his biography, Mark Twain wrote, "There are three kinds of lies: lies, damn lies, and statistics." He credited Benjamin Disraeli for the phrase but it is true that we need to look beyond how media portrays stats if we want to do good service to our readers.

Consider these two examples:

"51% of women would buy a red car if they purchased one today." Possible interpretations: "Most women would buy a red car if they purchased one today." or "More than half of all women would buy a red car if they purchased one today." or "Almost half of all women said they would buy anything but a red car if they purchased a car today."

This statistic can be interpreted several ways which confuses the reader as to how many women would buy a red car if they purchased one today.

"Two out of three dentists recommend toothpaste A".

Who is that third dentist? Faulty research methodology, such as a limited sample size or surveying only people in a certain geographic area, can also lead an author and therefore a reader to interpret statistics incorrectly.

Three strategies for using academic research effectively:
- If a news source directs you to "a recent study states…", track down the actual research before repeating it in your book.
- Hire a student to find relevant academic research at the university they attend.
- Conduct your own research with focus groups, surveys or interviews.

Clients' stories

Ask your clients about their challenges with the topic of your book. Some questions that may resonate are:
- What is your burning curiosity about this issue?
- When you think about this, what is the one thing that gets you upset?
- What do you really want to know about this?

Your experiences

Do you have further anecdotes, examples or metaphors that would illuminate and illustrate the points you wish to make?

Step Three: Research
Through the Author Personality

1. introvert or extravert?
2. pressure-prompted or pleasure-prompted?
3. linear or lateral thinker?
4. early bird or night owl?

Does your Author Personality affect how you approach Step Three: Research? If so, how?

_____
_____
_____
_____

Balancing the Milking Stool Roles

- Marketer/Entrepreneur or ME
- Manager/Administrator or MA
- Writer/Author or WA

Consider the publishing tasks that are listed at the beginning of Chapter 8. Which tasks of each role do you wish to take on in this step? Which tasks of this step should you partner with others, ask for help or hire out?

_____
_____
_____
_____

13
STEP FOUR
CHUNK OR OUTLINE

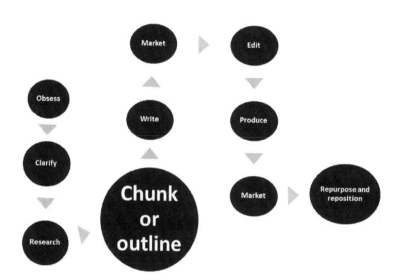

Once you have clarified your vision and have begun gathering your research, you are faced with the decision of what to do with it all.

Do you organize your material into logical sequence or do you chunk it into piles?

You may have heard the idea from other author coaches to purchase a binder, identify a tab for each chapter and then begin placing the information behind the appropriate tab. If you are a linear thinker, the binder strategy may be quite a useful tool. File folders, dutifully labeled and put neatly into a file cabinet is a similar system. Both ideas seem very logical and organized. And work very well for ladders.

Ladders begin writing by taking out the content behind Tab One or the first file folder and they begin to write chapter one.

However, if you are a kangaroo, the strategy above may very well derail your efforts. You may not immediately know where the content will reside in your new book, but don't let what seems like indecision demotivate you or stop you from moving forward. It is unnecessary for you to have tabs or files, in order or otherwise, to begin writing your first chapter.

A kangaroo's typical way of sorting research may be in piles instead of files. A kangaroo might have piles of paper on desks, on tables, on chairs, even on the floor. If you are a kangaroo, you may not know which pieces of paper will stay in what pile or if they will need to move over to another pile. Do not be concerned with assigning your research to a chapter pile, only a pile of main areas of focus.

Surrounded by piles

While ladders can easily put the research they are not immediately working with away in a filing cabinet, kangaroos might be more effective with the piles of research surrounding them like floating deck chairs after the sinking of the Titanic. While the piles may not be labeled as a specific chapter, it is useful to still identify the general concept. Try sticking a colored sticky note on each pile with the general area of focus. For example, when I was working on my book, *War and Peace in the Workplace*, three of the sticky notes read: visible minorities, gender, and night owls.

Pick a Pile

In the musical, *The Sound of Music*, Maria sings, "Let's start at the very beginning, a very good place to start." Maria is correct – if you are a ladder. Ladders will be best served by beginning with Chapter One as their first chapter.

For kangaroos, when you successfully start writing your book, it will rarely be with Chapter One. If you've been listening to a coach who says, "You start with Chapter One" or you have Maria's voice in your head from childhood, you may get stuck. Kangaroos will be best served by beginning their first chapter with a random pile of research.

Start with a pile and work on that chapter. When you are finished the chapter, you will likely have a list of research that you have included that you need to verify and pieces of research that you have decided not to include. Place the unused research pieces into other piles that are closely related. When the book is complete, you will need to decide which pieces of remaining research are completely irrelevant and should be abandoned and which pieces of research are of value and should be put aside for another book or writing project. Kangaroos are holistic and random in the sense they can start anywhere and finish anywhere.

No step in the Book Project model is more impacted by the lateral/linear part of our Author Personality.

Step Four: Chunk or Outline
Through the Author Personality

1. introvert or extravert?
2. pressure-prompted or pleasure-prompted?
3. linear or lateral thinker?
4. early bird or night owl?

Does your Author Personality affect how you approach Step Four: Chunk or Outline? If so, how?

_____

_____

_____

_____

Balancing the Milking Stool Roles

- Marketer/Entrepreneur or ME
- Manager/Administrator or MA
- Writer/Author or WA

Consider the publishing tasks that are listed at the beginning of Chapter 8. Which tasks of each role do you wish to take on in this step? Which tasks of this step should you partner with others, ask for help or hire out?

_____

_____

_____

_____

14
STEP FIVE
WRITE

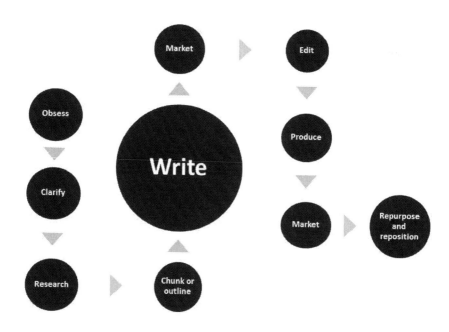

Dave Eggers, author of the books *A Heartbreaking Work of Staggering Genius* and *How We are Hungry,* is co-founder of 826 National, a network of creative writing and tutoring centers. He said, "The two things that stunt kids more than anything else are the fear that whatever they want to write about won't be acceptable, or that their first drafts have to be perfect." Isn't that what stunts adult writers as well?

As I write this chapter, I am twitching to go back and work on earlier chapters. But I know that the most important thing is to get it all out once, even the annoying chapter on the purpose of an index. Only when I have the first draft written, can I give myself permission to dwell in the land of perfection and return to the beginning.

There are many writers, fiction and non-fiction, who dwell so long in the land of the perfect Chapter One they never move beyond. Writing is about putting one page after the next and moving through the document. As we discussed in the opening chapters on Author Personality, the best way to move through the document is to understand and respect your Author Personality. Consider these questions: Where do you write, when do you write, and how long do you write?

Where do you write?

I believe in taking advantage of other people's real estate. Although I wrote my first book in my office, putting my unrelated papers and files in storage in a locked room, my second book was written in the rose garden of my friend's Vancouver home. My third book was written at my brother's grain farm in southern Saskatchewan and my fourth was written in a Mediterranean condo in Malta overlooking the ancient city of Mdina.

Is it necessary to go away? For me it is, but not for everyone. You may be lucky to have friends or family that will give you extended time in a quiet space to write, but perhaps your loved ones will not tolerate that level of desertion. Can you only be away for two days at a time? Or even, merely two hours at a time? The key is to find your preference and create a strategy to ensure you can focus. Find that place that makes sense for you.

Earlier in this book, we discussed the places you can work depending on your extravert and introvert predispositions.

Carl Hiaasen, author of numerous books including *Bad Monkey* and *Lucky*, recognizes the absolute aloneness he requires for his writing. "The first thing you see out of my office is a doormat that says: LEAVE. My wife got it for me, and it works pretty well."

Some introverts like to work in libraries. Some introverts go and rent an office space separate from their own. Think about where you would be the most productive and respect that preference.

When and how long do you write?

In chapter six on early birds and night owls, you had the opportunity to identify your circadian rhythm. When I hear an author claim that they get up at five a.m. and write for 40 minutes each day, I sigh. As an intermediate, my brain might kick in by eight a.m. but five a.m. is simply not a useful time for me to be doing anything that requires creative or intellectual capital. I can drag myself through the shower and to an airport at that time of day, but that is about it.

Understanding when you are most productive and creative is essential if you wish to write a great book quickly and stress-free.

How long you spend writing your book at one time is as important as the time of day you write. When you are a writer, as opposed to an author, you can focus in short bursts on a writing piece such as an article, blog post, or white paper. You certainly can do that type of writing for an hour or half an hour a day almost anytime during the day and achieve the required level of competence.

For many of us, writing a book is different. An author may require a continuous writing process until the first draft is finished. For many authors to be creatively productive, if they take a day off from writing, they will need time to reacquaint themselves with the document before they can move forward. Some authors find that one day away from the writing process requires them to invest an additional three days before they are fully back into the process. You need to identify and respect how you are affected by breaks and the time needed to get back into full gear.

How frequently you write, how long you write and what time of the day you write are often driven by the people in our lives. You don't want your family hating you because of this book. At the end of the book when you say, "Oh, that was a lot of work", you want your loved ones to say, "Congratulations!" not "Finally!"

Cracking Author's Block

We write every day, so it isn't so much writer's block as author's block that we are afraid of. Below are five fool-proof strategies to move out of that debilitating place some authors fall into and can't escape: follow a model, research, find your fans, write a different chapter and work on the yada yada.

Follow a Model
Steve Lowell, who mentors professional speakers, taught me a model for a keynote speech. As soon as learned the model, I realized that it would apply to writing a non-fiction book as well. Here are the steps, applied to a book project, that may propel you back into your process:
- What (premise of your book, build rapport with your reader, what do you promise they will know or learn in the book)
- Begin your story (this is particularly important if you are telling your story as the core of the book - your experience winning an Olympic medal, climbing Everest, starting a medical clinic in Afghanistan)
- Why (what are your reasons for writing the book and what are your readers' reasons for reading it)
- Why not (why you haven't been able to solve this problem in the past, why the reader hasn't been able to solve this problem

in the past)
- Middle part of your story (you made a decision to do something differently)
- How (most of the book is here – what are the models, steps, processes you want to introduce to the reader)
- The end of the story (what you discovered, learned and have resolved to do differently)
- What if you don't (what if you don't change, what if your reader doesn't change or adopt this new thinking/process/idea, what are the negative consequences)
- What if you do (what if you do change, what if your reader does change, what are the positive consequences)
- What is next? (issue your readers a challenge)
- What now? (issue a call to action to your readers)

Research

Researching is not writing. It is gathering data, notes, thoughts, quotes, stats – but it is not transforming those pieces into wisdom. That is writing. To push back author's block, revisit your research or discover new pieces to add to the project. Often this act gets your creative juices flowing once more.

Find your fans

This strategy is especially a good tool for extraverts as they tend to like to discuss ideas with others. Get feedback on your ideas from a family member, friend or colleague. Pick up the phone, call by Skype or meet in person to verbalize an idea that you are struggling with.

Write a different chapter

If you are a linear thinker, you may be stuck in a current chapter and want to finish it before you move on to the next. If you are writing non-fiction, choose another chapter to focus on and attempt to write on that topic before going back to the chapter you are struggling with.

Work on the yada yada

Writers are often so focused on the core content of a book (the introduction to the last chapter) that they ignore the back material, front material and cover content until the book is finished. By focusing on these other areas, which I call the yada yada, the author can give her mind a rest and come back to the project the next day with renewed creativity for the core content.

Step Five: Write
Through the Author Personality

1. introvert or extravert?
2. pressure-prompted or pleasure-prompted?
3. linear or lateral thinker?
4. early bird or night owl?

Does your Author Personality affect how you approach Step Five: Write? If so, how?

_____

_____

_____

_____

Balancing the Milking Stool Roles

- Marketer/Entrepreneur or ME
- Manager/Administrator or MA
- Writer/Author or WA

Consider the publishing tasks that are listed at the beginning of Chapter 8. Which tasks of each role do you wish to take on in this step? Which tasks of this step should you partner with others, ask for help or hire out?

_____

_____

_____

_____

15

STEP SIX MARKET

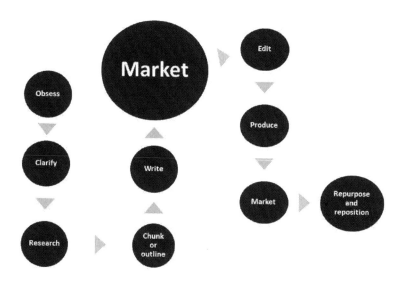

Few people that I know have done a bookstore book signing and exclaimed, "That's the most exciting thing that has ever happened in my life!" If they do, it is because friends and family flocked to the event and showered them with compliments, autograph requests and drove up the book signings total sales.

Unless you are Colin Powell, J.K.Rowling or Malcolm Gladwell, it is more likely that your experience will be one of lonely winsomeness, where you attempt to gain eye contact with bookstore shoppers and charm them over to your book signing table (which may very well be tucked away between tea pots and fantasy games). Even for extraverts, book signings can be tough.

To minimize your stress over the marketing of your book, it is important to redirect your attention to preliminary marketing as soon as you have finished your first draft and it is with your editors. Whether you go forward to organize book launches, signings and media appearances at the next marketing stage or not, insert your first marketing efforts at this step in the Book Project Model.

The marketing items to consider at this stage are media appearances, book launches and book signings. These are the events that cannot be organized quickly. Some stores require several months' notice for a book signing and if you choose to do a book launch, preliminary decisions need to be made now. Also as you talk to others about your book, they will wonder if you are doing media, launches or signings, and you will want to be able to answer those inquiries.

Book launches versus book signings

For the purpose of this discussion, let us first define book signings and book launches. A book signing is a low-key bookstore affair where the author sits and sign books after readers purchase the book and request the author's autograph. A book launch is usually not at a bookstore (although some independent bookstores offer them). There are usually beverages and food and a less somber and quiet atmosphere.

At a book signing, the author often has little or no control as to where in the store the book signing is located, what date and time the event will occur or what advertising or promotion the bookstore will provide. A book launch is under the control of the author and the question is really, how much money do you want to spend to launch this book? A facility, beverages, food and advertising all add to the budget.

Both events put you as the author front and center and this can be very stressful. You need to ask yourself: Can you do book launches, signings, and media or will these events give you heart palpitations?

If you decide to go forward, consider the strategies below.

Book signings

Self-published authors who primarily engage in book signings to make book sales are primed to be disappointed. Book stores are moving more and more to 'day stock' book signings which means the author brings in their product, sells it during the signing and then takes home the unsold books. The bookstore doesn't even enter the product into their system. You could make more sales sitting at home in your pajamas contacting people through social media. The book store takes a healthy commission (up to 45%) and so if you do not have a good margin, you may be selling your books at a loss.

Authors engage in book signings for two reasons: to have an event which they can contact media to promote and to be able to tell book buyers that their book is in Barnes and Noble or Chapters so the buyer is comfortable purchasing the author's book on line or directly from the author.

To pull off the most successful book store signing, consider these strategies:

- Contact all your close friends, family and colleagues in the area and let them know about the event. If they have already purchased the book, ask them to join you regardless. Try, "You probably have already purchased the book, but I would love for you to come down and chat, because doing a book signing can be lonely."

- Ask one good friend or family member to visit with you for the several hours of the event. When you are alone, your friend stands by your signing table and chats. If a person walks by and looks remotely interested in your book or speaking to you, your friend quietly slinks away and returns when you are alone once more. No one wants to come and talk to a lonely author, but if they see others are chatting the author up, they may take that as a sign that the book is interesting.
- Never read a book while you are at a signing, even your own. Introverts will not interrupt you and unless extraverts are keen for a chat, they won't either.

Book launches

Authors host book launches for several reasons. As with bookstore signings, a launch becomes an event which the author can promote through media. It is also an event to thank editors and contributors to the author's success. To pull off a low stress launch, consider these strategies:

- Find one or two other authors who have a different market and book focus for their new book and ask them to join you in a co-launch. Not only does this increase attendance and share the costs, the other authors' guests might have already bought their friend's book, but they probably have not heard about yours. You sell books to their guests, and they sell to yours. Your ideas are exposed to the other authors' colleagues and if you are a speaker, trainer or consultant, this could lead to new business.

- Develop a 10 minute presentation using PowerPoint with the main points of your book. Ask the other authors to do the same. Then take questions from the audience after the authors speak.

Media appearances

At this stage in the Book Project Model, consider what media appearances you would like to make once the book is in your hands. Construct a media list of print media, radio and local television and contact them to find out how they best like to work with local authors.

This gives producers the heads up about your book and then when you contact them later, you have already begun to build rapport, which makes ongoing communication more comfortable for all concerned.

Step Six: Market (Round One)
Through the Author Personality

1. introvert or extravert?
2. pressure-prompted or pleasure-prompted?
3. linear or lateral thinker?
4. early bird or night owl?

Does your Author Personality affect how you approach Step Six: Market? If so, how?

_____
_____
_____
_____

Balancing the Milking Stool Roles

- Marketer/Entrepreneur or ME
- Manager/Administrator or MA
- Writer/Author or WA

Consider the publishing tasks that are listed at the beginning of Chapter 8. Which tasks of each role do you wish to take on in this step? Which tasks of this step should you partner with others, ask for help or hire out?

_____
_____
_____
_____

16

STEP SEVEN
EDIT

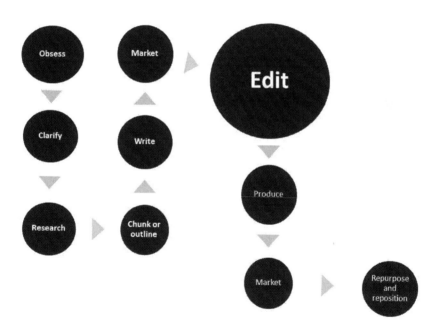

To ensure the best quality book, you need editors. Any author who thinks she can edit her own book is a fool.

Editors edit for content, readability, impact, spelling and grammar, and expert content. Since my first book, I have been lucky to have found colleagues, friends and family with great writing and editing skills who have acted as volunteer editors. All for the price of a book launch party, acknowledgement in the book and a lunch out. A few of my volunteer editors cover off one or two editing areas, while others address them all.

Let's explore each area:

Content
- Are the resources authoritative, are the original research methods competent, and are opinions supported by information?
- Are the facts organized and examined, not just listed? Are difficult concepts made manageable and is there a clear overview of the subject?
- Is the content fresh, innovative and insightful, and does it go beyond typical information on the subject?

Readability
- Does the material engage the reader and motivate the reader to finish the book?
- Is it free of jargon that the reader may not be familiar with?
- Is the tone of the book intelligent, but conversational?
- Does the author use examples, anecdotes, and wittiness when appropriate?

Impact
- Does the book teach without preaching?
- Does it leave the reader with solid benefit for the time and money invested in purchasing and reading the book?

Spelling and Grammar
- Spelling should be something that you catch as you write. Like grammar, the more you read the better speller you become.

However, be careful of the demon spellcheck as you may end up with hetereographs (where words share the same pronunciation but not the same spelling or meaning) such as they're, their and there. Editors will undoubtedly find misspelled words that the author has overlooked, even after multiple views by the writer.

Expert content

- These are people you ask to edit a specific chapter or group of chapters because either you have interviewed them for the chapter or they are an expert in the area.
- Whenever you have a complicated content chapter, ask yourself who you know that could give you feedback on that chapter?

You might be surprised that many people do not see editing a chapter or even the entire book as a chore, but a privilege. Most people want to be part of your project if they like you as a person. They want you to be successful. It seems like a big thing for you to ask them, but often it's not a big thing for them to take it on.

Guidelines for Author-Editor Relationships

- Ask nicely – they are doing you a favor.

- Be clear on exactly what you wish them to edit.

- Give the editors the document in whatever form they wish (PDF, word document, printed on paper) and take their input in whatever form they wish to provide it.

- Taking feedback is a challenge for many authors. Do not argue with any feedback, but ask for more information if you are not clear as to why they made the change recommendation to the manuscript.

- If more than one editor identifies an area of your book as needing a change, rethink your content. Ask what the editor sees as the issue. For example, are you not being clear enough, does your research not back up a statement, have you said something in an acerbic or disrespectful way?

- If you've asked an expert to edit a chapter, take their feedback very seriously.

- Getting negative feedback about anything is tough. The important thing is to focus on feedback, positive or negative, that helps you write a better book. If the feedback you received from a particular editor does not assist you in improving the book, it is not useful. You can either direct the editor as to how you would like feedback in the future, or perhaps not ask them to help you on your next book.

Step Seven: Edit
Through the Author Personality

1. introvert or extravert?
2. pressure-prompted or pleasure-prompted?
3. linear or lateral thinker?
4. early bird or night owl?

Does your Author Personality affect how you approach Step Seven: Edit? If so, how?

_____
_____
_____
_____

Balancing the Milking Stool Roles

- Marketer/Entrepreneur or ME
- Manager/Administrator or MA
- Writer/Author or WA

Consider the publishing tasks that are listed at the beginning of Chapter 8. Which tasks of each role do you wish to take on in this step? Which tasks of this step should you partner with others, ask for help or hire out?

_____
_____
_____
_____

17
STEP EIGHT
PRODUCE

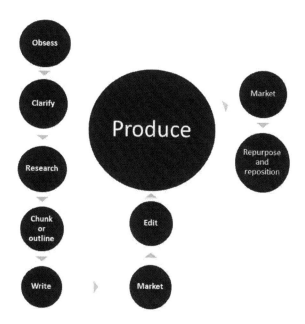

It is important in the clarify stage to determine who you are selling the book to, what kind of book it is and how will you sell it.

Size

If you are writing a book that will sell as a gift book in gift shops, you are not held to the strict sizing that a business book would require.

For business and issue related books, the size your buyers expect is the same as the other business books on your bookshelf, with good quality white interior paper stock. Do not deviate from this standard as it will confuse your buyers.

Fonts

Interior fonts should be serif (not sans serif such as Arial). I recommend Garamond 12 point or Bookman Old Style 10 or 11 point. These are both round letter fonts which makes reading easier. Choose sans serif fonts for eBooks and serif fonts for printed books. Ds

This book is printed in 12 Garamond.

Printing

If you are self-publishing, unless you have a client willing to take 3000 books or more, search out a print on demand supplier close to you or use the CreateSpace process.

CreateSpace is Amazon's new print on demand system. The author (or someone the author has hired) uploads the books' content and cover art in PDF format. From there, it is reasonably easy to format an eBook version for Kindle using the CreateSpace software.

When a customer purchases your book through Amazon.com (if you have produced the book through CreateSpace), Amazon ships the customer the book then and sends you your percentage as the author and publisher. It is that simple.

This means there is no more shipping books from your basement. If you do wish to obtain printed books you have authored for yourself, you can purchase stock through CreateSpace at a very reasonable price break, creating a good profit margin for books you sell directly to your readers. Ensure that you purchase through the CreateSpace site not Amazon to guarantee the author price discount.

Cover Design

For book covers, authors have choices that range from absolutely free to thousands of dollars. If you are using CreateSpace (as I did with this book cover), you can use their templates for free.

Alternatively, you may want something more complex or appropriate to the look you are trying to achieve with your book. Consider hiring a graphic designer. This can be done locally or at very price effectively through **www.fiverr.com** or **www.esource.com**.

Your Manager/Administrator takes on most of the tasks of this step.

Step Eight: Produce
Through the Author Personality

1. introvert or extravert?
2. pressure-prompted or pleasure-prompted?
3. linear or lateral thinker?
4. early bird or night owl?

Does your Author Personality affect how you approach Step Eight: Produce? If so, how?

_____
_____
_____
_____

Balancing the Milking Stool Roles

- Marketer/Entrepreneur or ME
- Manager/Administrator or MA
- Writer/Author or WA

Consider the publishing tasks that are listed at the beginning of Chapter 8. Which tasks of each role do you wish to take on in this step? Which tasks of this step should you partner with others, ask for help or hire out?

_____
_____
_____
_____

18
STEP NINE
MARKET II

Marketing your new book requires a marketing plan. At step six, you began thinking about your strategy and made some preliminary decisions. Let's look at those and other marketing ideas for your new book.

Book signings

Once you have your books with the editors, you have a good idea when the book will be available for bookstore signings and distributing to purchasers. Introverts might find book store signings more challenging than extraverts, but as mentioned earlier, few authors find signings entertaining.

Start with your community and once you have booked your local stores, reach out to other stores in the same chain, mentioning that you already have a signing booked at one of their locations. It will be easier to obtain a signing locally as most stores have a predisposition for local authors. My preference is to look first to independent book shops as they are more likely to have an author-friendly focus and will do more promotion on behalf of your book.

Book launch

If you decide to spend the time and money to organize a launch, start early in determining your guest list and sending out invitations. Check out other ideas under Step Six: Market.

Sales through social media

Once you have your book available, immediately send out announcements to contacts on social media. There are many actions you can take for this strategy, here are three:

- If you are selling through *Amazon*, design an author page on their site.
- Post a beginning chapter in the 'post' section of LinkedIn with links to your website or where the book can be purchased.
- Post in any groups you belong to on Facebook with a chapter teaser.

Your book as a primary marketing piece

Consider your new book as your primary marketing piece. If you are a speaker, trainer, consultant or coach, you have discovered that marketing brochures can cost several dollars each. For a few dollars more, you can give potential clients a free book. Unlike your brochure, your book will not be tossed in the trash. Because your book has longevity, ensure that your back pages have all the marketing materials that you would otherwise have in a brochure.

Your book in your pocket

Always carry a box of books in your car and one copy on your person. When you are at the airport, the dentist's office or going to a networking luncheon – be like American Express and don't leave home without it. An opportunity to sell the book or use it as a springboard into other business discussions may occur if you are prepared.

Cover cards

Print a business card with one side having the book cover and the other the title showing the website where it can be purchased, the author name and a one line promise of the value found in your book. For example, this book's one line promise could be, "Write your non-fiction book with less time, money and frustration."

Media

Some books are more newsworthy than others. The smaller the radio and television station, the more likely you will get on air. Generally print media is very difficult to get, however most communities have a weekly newspaper which often has an author page for local books.

Ask yourself, what are the controversial or contraindicative elements of your book? Can you tie any parts of your book to current news issues? Use those points in news releases.

Dripping on your database

If you send out information regularly as a blog, email article, or newsletter, begin adding your book onto the bottom of each issue for the three or four issues prior to the release. "Here's my new book, it's coming out March 1st. It will be available at the following locations (list stores, sites and any book signings)."

Client bulk discounts

"At the bookstore, the new book will be $20.99. As a client, I can send you this new book at a 50% reduction if you buy 20 or more for the people in your organization." I sold 2000 copies of my second book, *Escape from Oz*, before the book was printed with this strategy alone.

Book awards

Investigate your local and regional book award programs and their application deadlines. The great thing about book awards is that it doesn't matter if you win, what matters is being shortlisted. The shortlist is where the publicity is. It is the shortlist that is in the media and the award night's marketing material. It is nice to win, but it is the shortlist that counts.

If you are thinking they seldom give awards to self-published authors, you are correct. They rarely do, but your goal is the shortlist, so don't let the outcome of win or lose stop you from entering.

Back of the room sales

Leave a stack of books at the back table where people are flowing out of the room after your presentation. If they enjoyed your presentation, they want more information. Leave a sign, "Throw in a $20 and take a book. If you want it autographed, please see me later." In 23 years, only two of my books have been stolen.

Like the book signings, you want to make it as easy as possible for people to buy from you and as stress-free as possible for you to sell.

More books

Have a new book to move sales of your previous titles. When people see you have a book, the decision they make is, "Should I buy the book nor not?" When you have two books, the decision they have to make, "Should I buy the first book or the second one?" Each time I bring out a new book, I have an increase of sales on the previous books. People want choice.

Step Nine: Market – Round Two
Through the Author Personality

1. introvert or extravert?
2. pressure-prompted or pleasure-prompted?
3. linear or lateral thinker?
4. early bird or night owl?

Does your Author Personality affect how you approach Step Nine: Market? If so, how?

_____
_____
_____
_____

Balancing the Milking Stool Roles

- Marketer/Entrepreneur or ME
- Manager/Administrator or MA
- Writer/Author or WA

Consider the publishing tasks that are listed at the beginning of Chapter 8. Which tasks of each role do you wish to take on in this step? Which tasks of this step should you partner with others, ask for help or hire out?

_____
_____
_____
_____

19

STEP TEN
REPURPOSE AND
REPOSITION

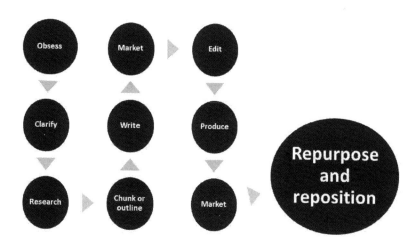

You have struggled to research, write and produce this book in physical form. Once you have it in your hot little hands, ask yourself, "How else can I use this material?" Let me give you some examples:

Articles and blogs

My graduate research was on how criminal and corporate leaders are similar and different. I interviewed social workers, probation officers and corrections workers to understand the gang leaders they had as clients and inmates. This material provided the basis for my graduate thesis – a piece of work that no one read with the exception of other students writing on similar subjects for their graduate or post-graduate work. I repurposed my thesis material into a chapter for the book *Leading in Complex Worlds* which is a peer-reviewed international leadership journal. I later repurposed the chapter into a white paper and a series of articles which I sent out to my database of clients over a period of several months.

If you provide material on a regular basis to your clients through articles or blogs, your book will give you months of good content. Just take an idea from your book and add a concluding paragraph

eBooks

For many reasons, many people still prefer the physical book. Even Sheryl Sandberg, COO of Facebook and author of the book *Lean In*, said, "I probably shouldn't admit this since I work in the tech industry, but I still prefer reading paper books. I travel with an iPad, but at home I like holding a book open and being able to leaf through it, highlight with a real yellow pen, and dog-ear important pages. After I finish a book, I'll often look to see how many page corners are turned down as one gauge of how much I liked it. I tried the Kindle app for the iPad on the elliptical, but when you get sweaty, you can't turn the pages."

It doesn't matter whether you have a personal preference such as Sandberg regarding printed books. At the end of the day, she too published her book as an eBook along with a print edition. EBooks are essential in today's market and authors who believe that eBooks are somehow beneath them are, as the saying goes, biting off their nose to spite their face. EBooks are essential in today's market.

For those readers who have embraced the EBook, don't miss the opportunity to get the electronic copy of your book in their hands. Either do the necessary research to engage in KOBO, KINDLE and NOOK, or hire it out.

This is an area where your Manager/Administrator needs to take a lead role.

Audio Books and iTunes

My first three books were professionally recorded, mastered and reproduced. Although they are not as big sellers as the print and eBook formats, there is a market for the traveler who wants to listen instead of read. And let's not forget all those elliptical machines.

With the popularity of iTunes, you may also consider loading your audio files into iTunes and selling them for a small amount per chapter.

Step Ten: Repurpose and Reposition Through the Author Personality

1. introvert or extravert?
2. pressure-prompted or pleasure-prompted?
3. linear or lateral thinker?
4. early bird or night owl?

Does your Author Personality affect how you approach Step Nine: Repurpose and Reposition? If so, how?

_____
_____
_____
_____

Balancing the Milking Stool Roles

- Marketer/Entrepreneur or ME
- Manager/Administrator or MA
- Writer/Author or WA

Consider the publishing tasks that are listed at the beginning of Chapter 8. Which tasks of each role do you wish to take on in this step? Which tasks of this step should you partner with others, ask for help or hire out?

_____
_____
_____
_____

20

THE YADA YADA

With the last word of the last chapter, The Writer/Author happily releases her mouse, steps away from the computer, throws her hands in the air and cries, "It is done!"

But the Marketer/Entrepreneur interrupts, "Just a minute, what about the front and back pages, and the cover? This book can't go out naked into the world. It needs to sell its image."

The Manager/Administrator mumbles, "Where are the back pages for bulk buying information? The Library of Congress information?"

The Writer/Author waves her hand in a dismissing tone to her fellow roles of ME and MA and mumbles, "Oh, yada yada."

According to the Oxford English Dictionary, 'yada yada' indicates, in a dismissive way, 'Trivial, meaningless, or uninteresting talk or writing; chatter'. However for self-published writers, the yada

yada is a golden opportunity to promote the writer, the publisher and the book.

So what is the yada yada of a non-fiction book? It is the front pages, back pages, front cover, book spine and back cover. The yada yada tells the reader about the book itself and you, the author.

21

THE COVER

Once a physical non-fiction book is in his hand, the typical buyer peruses the book in this order:

1. looks at the front cover
2. flips the book over to peruse the back cover
3. opens up the front pages to read the table of contents
4. flips through the book, stopping briefly at graphics
5. turns to the back pages to find the index to see the terms that might relate to their interest
6. reviews the core content of the book.

For an eBook, the process is similar . The prospective purchaser looks at the cover on line, and then reads the 'back cover content' usually placed on the bottom of the online listing. If there is preview option, the prospective buyer 'opens' the book and reads the table of contents and then any other pages included in the preview.

This is why putting an appropriate amount of preview pages in an eBook listing is important. The preview needs to compensate for the potential buyer being unable to flip through the pages of the entire book.

Front cover design

The essentials of the front cover are the image, author name, and book title/subtitle. There is some debate as to whether seeing anything but those three elements detract from or add to the book's appeal for the buyer, but the most important thing is that your front cover should draw your reader in from three feet away with legible fonts and good color contrast. The greatest title in the world will be lost without legibility and colour contrast.

On this book cover, I included the essentials above as well as a front book quote. A front book quote can be from you as the author or from a person known to the readers as an authority or celebrity. "Write your non-fiction book now!" is a useful quote as an author quote because my main title/subtitle does not mention writing or non-fiction. This is an area where you can reveal your promise as to what the book delivers if the title is not as precise.

Spine design

A spine contains minimally the title and author name and can also contain the subtitle and publisher imprint. Remember that on book shelves, your book is rarely face forward and is most likely spine forward, so the spine is the first thing the buyer sees. The title must be as legible as possible to attract the notice of the browser.

If you are using a template system like CreateSpace or using an assisted-publishing agency, you may not be in control of the spine design.

Back cover design

The back cover minimally contains the ISBN code, a paragraph about the book, and a paragraph about the author. It can also contain testimonials about the book, the author's picture, or a quote from the book.

Book content bleep

Your book paragraph, also known as your book bleep, should answer the questions: what, how and why. What is the problem the reader is experiencing? How will your book address that problem? Why should they care, what is in it for them?

For example, this book's bleep is:

Not moving forward on your non-fiction book writing project? Too much advice from too many people but none of it seems to work for you? The first step to success as an author is to identify your Author Personality. With this knowledge, you can save yourself frustration, time and money. Find the answers to the key questions that determine your Author Personality. Apply them to the ten step 'Obsess to Reposition' process that will ensure completion of your book!

Problem: Not moving forward on your non-fiction book writing project? Too much advice from too many people but none of it seems to work for you?
Solution: The first step to success as an author is to identify your Author Personality.
Benefit: With this knowledge, you can save yourself frustration, time and money.
Promise: Find the answers to the key questions that determine your Author Personality. Apply them to the ten step 'Obsess to Reposition' process that will ensure completion of your book!

Biographical author bleep

The author bleep is your opportunity to build credibility with your reader. You have established that the book will address their problem, now you need to convince them that you are the author qualified to share that information. The author bleep answers the question: Why you?

Jeanne Martinson, MA is a bestselling Canadian author of seven books (six non-fiction and one fiction). She has coached authors throughout Canada and the United States on the models revealed in this book. To learn more about Jeanne and her book coaching services, see **www.wooddragonbooks.com**.

Credentials that your buyers would recognize: Jeanne Martinson, MA
Proof of your experience: is a bestselling Canadian author of seven books (six non-fiction and one fiction). She has coached authors throughout Canada and the United States on the models revealed in this book.
Place to go for more: To learn more about Jeanne and her book coaching services, see **www.wooddragonbooks.com**.

ISBN

Introduced in 1970, The International Standard Book Number is a unique 13 digit numeric commercial book identifier assigned to each edition and variation of a book. The ISBN is 13 digits long if assigned on or after January 1st, 2007, and 10 digits long if assigned before 2007. The method of assigning an ISBN depends on the country in which the book is published. ISBN codes are essential if you wish to sell your book anywhere besides off your own website or back of the room at events.

In Canada, ISBNs are assigned by Library and Archives Canada and are free of charge. See **http://www.bac-lac.gc.ca/eng/services/isbn-canada/Pages/isbn-canada.aspx**. Other countries may vary.

In conclusion, whether you use a designer to design your cover or use a template, as I did with this book through CreateSpace, the above elements should be carefully considered to ensure the highest degree of appeal to your reader and buyer.

22

THE FRONT PAGES

The front pages must minimally include title page, copyright page with publishing information, and Table of Contents. It can also contain an autograph page, page of acknowledgements, note from the author, early praise for the book or the author's previous related books, information from the Library of Congress or Library of Canada, caveats, and a book dedication.

You will note that this book contains the three essential pages plus a caveats page, page of acknowledgements, note from the author and a book dedication.

Autograph Page

This is the first page in the book and where you sign your autograph for interested readers. Do not assume someone buying your book wants it autographed, or autographed to them. Ask before you waste a book.

The autograph page should only contain the main book title. It could also be blank.

The Title Page

The title page includes the full title, author and publishing imprint. As a self-published author, you may not have a publishing imprint. You may use your company logo if you are publishing through your own company. If you are using an assisted-publishing agency, they might print their imprint on this page.

Copyright Page

This usually resides on the backside of the Title Page. It minimally must contain the copyright of the author, an All Rights Reserved statement, acknowledgement of any copyrights or permissions used within the content, the publishing house information (which would be you if self-published), and the ISBN written in numbers. It can also include the printing location and Library of Congress or Library of Canada information which is essential to access library sales and library photocopy commissions.

Copyright can be written in full or with a small 'c' in a circle graphic followed by the author's name.

The All Rights Reserved statement tells readers that the author has legal rights to the material in the book and to please not steal the author's intellectual capital. There is no one perfect statement, so check out several books and draft one that you are comfortable with.

Copyrights of others must be acknowledged if you are using a considerable amount of copyrighted material and are not acknowledging that content use in the document itself. For example, if I was using Steve Lowell's model in *Chapter 14, Step Four: Write* word for word from his book, I would need to acknowledge he was the author of the content.

Publishing information is important to ensure that anyone who wishes to contact the author or publisher for media or book sales can find them easily. Don't make the potential buyers of your book search to find you.

Library of Congress and Library of Canada information is often essential to access library sales and therefore PLR payments and library photocopy commissions.

Public Lending Rights (PLR) payments are a form of passive income for authors. Throughout the world, governments acknowledge that when you sell a book to a library, many people who read your book access the content for free. The PLR system compensates authors for that income loss.

Libraries are surveyed annually for notice (or hits) of the books on its nation's registry and through a formula, it is determined what the payback to the author should be financially. Register your books both with your national library and with the PLR system and ensure your books are in libraries. Even if the library doesn't want to buy the book, having your book in their collection is your favour so consider donating a copy.

In Canada, the Canadian Council for the Arts administers the program. See **http://plr-dpp.ca/PLR/default.aspx** to find how to register your books.

Not only are books read by multiple readers, they are copied by multiple readers. In Canada, the organization known as Access Copyright ensures that authors are compensated for the multiple readers who are also copying book content. Institutions such as libraries and universities are required by law to pay for the privilege of copying and using published works. Access Copyright gathers these fees and distributes the funds to the creators of the published works.

To access this pool of funds, authors are required to register their books with Access Copyright. See **http://www.accesscopyright.ca/creators**.

Acknowledgements

This page can reside at the front or the back of the book. Ensure that you ask permission of anyone you thank on this page and what you thank them for.

Note From the Author

This supplementary non-core content is from the author and often explains why the author wrote this book at this particular time. Caveats can also be included in this section or in a separate section.

Caveats

Caveat pages are used to answer the 'why?' questions of your reader. For example, on my caveat page, I address "Why is she switching from male to female pronouns, why isn't she addressing traditional publishing?"

Table of Contents

This page is essential to the non-fiction book. If you wrote the core content and could only print one more page, it needs to be this one. A non-fiction book without a table of contents is like a mystery fiction book without a resolution to the crime. Simply not done.

Early Praise for the book

How will you get testimonials for the book before it is released? Ask anyone who read the book as an editor or an expert what they thought of the book and who do they thought the book would serve? If their comments are complimentary, ask them if you can use their quote in the front of the book or on the back cover.

Dedication

I have dedicated my previous non-fiction books to my father, to women who struggle in hostile lands and several to my husband, Malcolm. My fiction book was not dedicated. This book is dedicated to

P.D. James, a crime fiction writer. James helped me to understand how to move from non-fiction to fiction writing and the power of research. We were only acquaintances but she was a powerful force in my writing career over the last four years. She passed away November 27th, 2014.

23

THE BACK PAGES

After the Table of Contents, the most important added page is the Index. It is also the only essential element of the back pages. Other pages that can be added are: information about your business, previous books, biography of the author, bibliography or resources, upcoming books, and notes. You will note that I have included in the back pages of this book information about my businesses, previous books, my biography, a short resource list, and upcoming books. I did not include notes that I cited through the content as I went along.

Index

In our eBook world, some authors are eschewing indexes, believing that readers will simply go to the find button and insert the word they are looking for and locate it in the electronic document. However, that is not the most important reason we put indexes in non-fiction books. Like the table of contents, an index does assist the reader in finding specific information. But as the Marketer/Entrepreneur role should note, the table of contents and index are included primarily to help readers understand which concepts are addressed in the book so they can make a buying decision.

Information about your business

The back cover biography bleep should be narrowly focused to credibility items specific to the book. The back pages, however, allow the author to provide information regarding other services the author may provide, related to the content of the book or not. For example, I manage a training and speaking business in the area of diversity and leading diverse workplaces. The back pages would be an appropriate location to introduce both of my businesses.

Think through carefully what you should add if you have multiple business streams. Do they complement each other or confuse the reader? For example, if this was a book on writing mystery fiction, including business consulting services at the end of the book would be very confusing. The reader would ask, "Why is that here?" Where many of my readers for this book will be consultants, coaches, speakers and trainers, the link to my diversity business is logical, but they are not necessarily my core buying group for diversity services.

How can I talk about all the services I provide while being concise, appropriate and effective? To that end, I have included my diversity business credentials in my biography and have included my non-fiction books in the 'Books by the Author' section, but have not included information regarding my diversity consulting services under 'Author Services'..

Previous books and upcoming books

This is the ideal space for introducing the reader to other books that you have authored, regardless of genre. In printed books, use cover graphics. In eBook editions, do not. In printed editions, if you have QR codes that take the reader instantly to a buying page, use those as well.

The descriptions following the title and graphics should follow the same format as the book bleep on the back cover of the book you are currently publishing.

Biography of the author

This is not the time to be shy, but neither is it time to fudge, fib, or puff up your real history. Focus on the elements that will help sell your book. In non-fiction, these are experience, education, achievements, awards, and previous books. Unless it is directly related, readers do not care about your pets, travels, spouses, sports, hobbies, or idiosyncrasies.

Bibliography or Resources

The bibliography and resources section are similar but not identical. A bibliography is a listing of books used as sources for the content in the book. A resources section can be a listing of sources used in the book, but they are just as likely to be a listing of sources for further or in-depth learning by the reader. For example under the resources section in this book, I mention two books on grammar which I have found particularly useful in my own writing. I also mention Stephen King's book on writing which was both a source for content and a source for new learning for the reader.

Endnotes, Footnotes and Notes

A footnote is a note at the end, or foot, of a page. An endnote is a note at the end of the chapter, section or book. A note is a note at the end of the book. If you quote someone, you should cite the author or speaker, creating a 'citation'. I cited the author or source of the material in this book as I went along, and therefore was not required to create endnotes, footnotes or notes.

23

THE END OF THE STORY

Once upon a time, three authors, John, Frank and Georgia, each dreamed about writing a book. But they struggled with starting and completing their projects, often getting stuck and feeling frustrated. But along the way, they discovered the three legs of the milking stool model, the ten steps of the Book Project Model and began to respect their individual Author Personalities.

Georgia, her friend Penny, John and Frank sat around a table at the end of the evening of the three authors' joint book launch. The three authors smiled. Their books had been launched successfully to a room of receptive colleagues, clients and friends. Each guest had purchased several books.

Georgia leaned back in her chair and sighed. "I like being an author." John and Frank high fived each other, their smiles broadening. Penny shook her head in disbelief, "I guess miracles really do happen."

The truth is you don't need a miracle to get your book written. You just need good models that help you create a process that respects your individuality and Author Personality!

The End

INDEX

Acknowledgements 129, 130, 131
Advance(s) 46, 52, 55-56
Allen Lane 54
Amazon 65, 71, 110, 114
Anchor 54
Appetite 54
Apollo 22
Assisted-publishing 3, 9, 52, 55, 58-59, 73, 126, 130
Audio books 79, 121
Autobiography 74-75

Ballantine 54
Bantam 54
Bentham, Jeremy 29-30
Biography 56, 74, 75, 127, 135-136
Blackford, Katherine 81, 82
Blonde 81, 82
Bond Street 54
Book awards 116, 137, 147
Book signings 29, 30, 46, 57, 86, 97-100, 114, 116-117, 128
Book launches 29, 47, 98-100, 103, 114, 139
Brunette 81-82
Bucholtz, Malcolm 73

Capote, Truman 17
Carroll, Lewis 17
Cochrane, Kristin 55
Compilation 74-75, 147
Copyright 129, 130, 131
Cover 53, 56, 68, 72, 73, 94, 104, 110, 111, 115, 123-126, 135-137
CreateSpace 46, 110-111, 126, 128
Credibility 55, 63-64, 126, 136

Dell 54
Dickens, Charles 17

Dionysus 22
Disraeli, Benjamin 82
Doubleday 54

Early bird 41-43, 77, 91
eBooks 58, 110, 120-121
Eggers, Dave 78
Emblem 54
Extroversion 21-22
Extavert 18, 21-27, 77, 91, 93, 98, 100, 114

Fonts 110, 126
Foot, David 73
Franklin, Benjamin 41
Freeman, Jean 75

Gerber, Michael 46
Gladwell, Malcolm 73-74, 81, 98

Hamish Hamilton 54
Hauter, Wenonah 73
Hemingway, Ernest 17, 18
Henry, Lynn 55
Hiaasen, Carl 9
Homer 91

Index 90, 125, 135
Intermediate 42-43, 91
Introversion 21-22
Introvert 26-27, 77, 91, 100, 114
ISBN 126, 128, 130
James, Florence Bean 75
James, PD 15, 132
Jung, Carl 21-22

Kangaroos 36-37, 86-87
Kindle 71, 110, 120, 121,
King, Stephen 15, 16, 137

141

Knopf 54

Ladders 36-37, 86-87
Kobo 71, 121
Lateral 35-37, 39, 40, 72-73, 77, 87
Legacy publisher 46, 51-56
Linear 39, 72-73, 77, 86-87, 93
Left brain 35-38
Lowell, Steve 92,130
Ludgate, Katherine 81

Manager/Administrator (MA) 47-49, 111, 121, 123, 128
Marketer/Entrepreneur (ME) 47-49, 123, 136
Martin , Brad55
McClelland & Stewart 54
MBTI 21, 26
Media 57-58, 62, 73, 81-82, 98-101, 114-116, 130
Memoir 74-75
Myers Briggs Type Indicator 21, 26

Newman, Toni 66
Night owl 42-43, 77, 87, 91
Nook 71, 121

Paterson, Donald 81
Penguin 54-55
Penguin Random House 54-55
Pleasure-prompted 18, 29-33, 72
Portfolio 54
Potter 54

Powell, Colin 98
Pressure-prompted 18, 29-33, 72
Putnam 54
Puffin 54
Random House 54-55
Right brain 35-38
Rowling, JK 98

Royalties 52, 56
Sandberg, Sheryl 120
Schur, Carolyn 42-43
Self-publishing 47, 51-53, 55, 58-59, 73, 99, 116, 123, 130,
Shaw, George Bernard 18
Sherrin, Joe 81
Signal 54
Sirolli, Ernesto 46
Spine 54, 124, 126

Thoreau, Henry David 27
Traditional publisher 46, 51-59, 132
Tundra 54
Twain, Mark 17, 51, 82

Viking 54
Vintage 54

WES 45
Wolfe, Thomas 17, 18
Women Entrepreneurs of Saskatchewan 45, 147
Woolf, Virginia 17
Writer/Author (WA) 47-49, 123

RESOURCES

I am recommending only two resources. There are many wonderful books to reference for your learning pleasure, but I thought if you were to only read two, they would be:

Grammar and Spelling

Say What? The Fiction Writer's Handy Guide to Grammar, Punctuation, and Word Usage
By C.S. Lakin
Although for fiction authors, I have used this great guide for non-fiction books to keep me clear on 'confusables' and odd grammar such as 'different from versus different than'. Very readable!

On Writing

On Writing: A Memoir of the Craft
by Stephen King
This is both a memoir of King's struggle to rise in publishing as well as a great guide to the inner mind of a successful author. Worth every minute you spend with it!

ABOUT THE AUTHOR

Jeanne Martinson, M.A. is a professional speaker, trainer and best-selling author who has worked internationally and throughout Canada. Since co-founding her own firm, MARTRAIN Corporate and Personal Development in 1993, Jeanne has inspired thousands of participants in her workshops and keynote presentations with her humor, insight and real-world examples.

Jeanne became interested in training while working for a Fortune 500 company in southern California. Back in her home province of Saskatchewan, she side-stepped into sales and marketing for ten years in the printing and labelling industry, where she took a $25,000 sales territory and grew it to $850,000 within four years.

Jeanne completed her Master of Arts degree in Leadership at Royal Roads University in Victoria, British Columbia, Canada. (Her graduate research focused on the differences and similarities of criminal gang leaders and corporate leaders). Jeanne also holds a Certificate in Organisational (Organizational) Behaviour from Heriot-Watt University (Edinburgh, Scotland) and is certified as a practitioner of NLP (Neuro Linguistic Programming).

As Managing Partner of her own firm, Jeanne delivers workshops and keynote addresses to government, associations and the private sector. Her most popular topics are leadership and diversity. As a Canadian bestselling author and strategist in workplace diversity, Jeanne's goal is to assist leaders in understanding diversity issues so they may attract, retain and engage their ideal workforce.

In July 1999, Jeanne released her first non-fiction book titled *Lies and Fairy Tales That Deny Women Happiness* which explores the myths that many Canadian women are raised with and which limit their ability to have happy relationships and fulfilling careers.

Her second book, *Escape from Oz – Leadership For The 21st Century* was released in October 2001. This book explores the parallels of the characters in the fable *The Wonderful Wizard of Oz* and our own beliefs about personal and professional leadership.

Jeanne's third book, *War & Peace in the Workplace – Diversity, Conflict, Understanding, Reconciliation* was released September 2005. This book explores how workplaces are becoming more diverse and how diversity may trigger conflict. The book illustrates how we have the choice of allowing conflict to spiral down into dysfunction or of taking charge, becoming aware and developing understanding.

Jeanne's fourth book was a chapter based on her graduate work in a larger compilation. Her research was published by the International Leadership Association in their annual journal (2012) as a peer-reviewed journal article (Leadership Lessons from the Criminal World).

Jeanne's fifth book, *Generation Y and the New Ethic*, was released Spring 2013. It gives concrete information about the four different generations found in the workplace today with a focus on work ethic and the motivations and values of Generation Y.

Jeanne's sixth book, *If it Wasn't for the Money*, is her first fiction novel and introduces her main character, Sam Anderson, a travel journalist and accidental murder detective. It was introduced in 2014.

Jeanne takes a leading role in her community, a dedication that was recognized with the awarding of the Canada 125 Medal, the YWCA Women of Distinction Award (Business, Labor and Professions), the Centennial Leadership Award (for outstanding contribution to the Province of Saskatchewan), the Athena Award, and the EMCY (the national Diversity award of Canada).

Jeanne has been listed in Who's Who of Canadian Women since 1996 and Canadian Who's Who since 1999. Jeanne is Past President of: Saskatchewan Training and Development Association (Regina Chapter), Saskatchewan Business and Professional Women, and Women Entrepreneurs of Saskatchewan. She was Founding President of the Saskatchewan Chapter of the Canadian Association of Professional Speakers (CAPS).

BOOKS BY JEANNE MARTINSON

If It Wasn't For the Money
Written by Jeanne Martinson
Under the name J.A. Martine
In print and eBook

    Sailing on a cruise ship to Alaska to discover unusual adventures to write about for her magazine, OOTA, journalist Sam Anderson gets caught up in the disappearance of a wealthy dining companion.

    Who could financially benefit from the death of the heiress? Travelling from the icy glaciers of Alaska to the steamy heat of New Orleans, Sam begins to tie up the loose strings of the mystery – but can she solve the puzzle before she too becomes a target?

    The first book in the series. The second book, **Stay out of the Water,** is due out February 2016.

Generation Y and the New Work Ethic
In print and eBook

Every generation has rebelled against the norms of the generation preceding it. This rebellion manifests itself externally in clothes, hairstyles, temporary and permanent markings and maskings. As time passes, often these visual distinctions are toned down or abandoned as that generation ages and begins to fit into mainstream work worlds, eventually falling for the tie and pantyhose cultural norms of the workplace. Many of today's Generation Y cohort members may yet desert their desire for flip-flops and casual attitudes as they progress in their careers and organizations.

Managers ask me frequently "When will Gen Ys will grow up, quit rebelling and get with the program?" Unfortunately for managers and co-workers everywhere, there is more to generational difference than rebellion and a desire to be different from the previous generation. Our

generational identity is also about the beliefs and values that were developed in our growing up years. By the time we hatch into the

workforce, our perspectives of others, work and the world are well formed.

So why are we talking about generational differences now more so than in the past? Why has this last generation upset the apple cart so significantly? Because it is the perfect storm!

If you are a colleague trying to understand your multi-generational co-workers, a front line manager trying to get your youngest workers to show up and show up on time, or are a member of Generation Y and looking for ways to maximize your effectiveness and success in the workplace, this book is for you. Jeanne Martinson gets to the heart of the generational differences issue, with minimal psychobabble and statistical navel gazing, giving you concrete information about the different generations with a focus on work ethic and the motivations and values of Generation Y.

Table of Contents

Introduction - Why is Generation Y so Different?
Chapter One - Defining the Generations
Chapter Two - The New Work Ethic
Chapter Three - The Loyal Traditionalists
Chapter Four - The Busy baby Boomers
Chapter Five - The Entrepreneurial Gen X
Chapter Six - The Newer Faster Generation Y
Chapter Seven - Why Occasionally None of this Matters
Chapter Eight - Why We Just Can't Get Along
Chapter Nine - Managing Generation Y
Chapter Ten - Workplace Strategies for Gen Y
Epilogue – A Letter to Leaders

Leading in Complex Worlds

Chapter 8 – Leadership Lessons from the Criminal World – written by Jeanne Martinson

In print format

"Leading in Complex Worlds" was released June 2012 by publisher Jossey-Bass. This collection of chapters from leadership experts and scholars is the annual peer-reviewed journal of the International Leadership Association. It contains chapters from fifteen authors, including a chapter by Jeanne Martinson titled "Leadership Lessons from the Criminal World" **which is based on her Master of Arts research project that compared criminal and corporate leaders.**

The other chapters include:

- Black Women's Political Leadership Development: Recentering the Leadership Discourse

- Soccer Tactics and Complexity Leadership

- The Role of Culture and History in the Applicability of Western Leadership Theories in Africa

- A Tao Complexity Tool, Leading from Being

- The Leadership of Dr. Jane Goodall: A Four Quadrant Perspective

Escape from Oz – Leadership for the 21st Century

by Jeanne Martinson

In print, audio book and eBook formats

"Escape From Oz – Leadership For The 21st Century" explores the parallels of the characters in the fable "The Wonderful Wizard of Oz" and our own beliefs about personal and professional *leadership*.

The first part of the book explores the four cornerstones required to be an effective leader: courage, insight, self-discipline and influence over others.

The second part of the book explores how we can move out of our comfort zone to lead individuals according to their reality, skill set and knowledge base – with the goal of achieving trust and long term success.

This book, about the basics of personal leadership and leading others, is written to assist you in becoming an effective leader – whether you are leading an organization of two or two thousand.

Table of Contents

Chapter One - A Leader – Who Me?
Chapter Two - Four Cornerstones of Personal Leadership

Chapter Three - The First Cornerstone: Insight
Chapter Four - The Second Cornerstone: Courage
Chapter Five - The Third Cornerstone: Self-Discipline
Chapter Six - The Fourth Cornerstone: Influence
Chapter Seven - Trust: The Glue of Leadership
Chapter Eight – The Stairway to 21st Century Leadership
Chapter Nine – Climbing the Stairs
Chapter Ten - Epilogue
Chapter Eleven – Leadership Principles

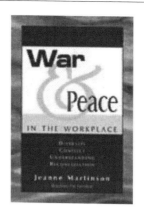

War & Peace – Diversity, Conflict, Understanding, Reconciliation

by Jeanne Martinson

In print, eBook and audio book formats

Wonder why we can't just get along? Why we react to each other the way we do?

Most conflict in the workplace comes from our differences – both our diversity in the big 'D' issues such as race, gender or ability but also diversity in the small 'd' issues such as values, marital and family status, age or thought processes. Diversity can be problematic and it can be wonderful. As individuals and organizations, we can benefit from the many perspectives that create the synergy to move an organization forward by leaps and bounds.

On the other hand, differences can bring conflict, toxic work groups, low morale, harassment, misunderstandings and employee turnover.

Many organizations adopt respectful workplace or harassment policies. But this isn't enough to realize the benefits of a diverse workforce or to minimize diversity-based conflict. We need to shift how we perceive and work with others. This book illustrates how we have the choice of allowing conflict to spiral down into dysfunction or of taking charge, becoming aware and developing understanding. It's all up to you!

Table of Contents

Chapter One - We Can't Ignore Diversity

AWARENESS
Chapter Two - What is Diversity Anyway?
Chapter Three - The Myth of Presumed Sameness
Chapter Four - Us and Them and We
Chapter Five - We Made It – Why Haven't They?
Chapter Six - We's Not Me's

UNDERSTANDING
Chapter Seven – From Nations to Tribes and Back Again (Aboriginal Issues)
Chapter Eight – Welcome to Barneyland (Immigration and Visible Minority Issues)
Chapter Nine – My Kind of Christian (Religion in the Workplace)
Chapter Ten – Crossing the Gender Divide
Chapter Eleven – Leaping the Generation Gaps (Traditionalists, Boomers, Gen Xers, Gen Ys)
Chapter Twelve – Perspectives on Time (Polychronic/Monochronic time, early bird/night owl)
Chapter Thirteen – The Other Brain (left brain/right brain issues)

RECONCILIATION
Chapter Fourteen – What Can I Do As An Individual?
Chapter Fifteen – What Can I Do As A Leader?
Chapter Sixteen – What Can We Do As An Organization?

SYNERGY

Chapter Seventeen - Why Should We Care?

Author Services

Do you think you need more assistance or coaching with your book writing project? We would love to help further.

The Big Review
A review of your manuscript with comments regarding title, grammar and spelling, flow, readability, and marketability.

Workshops
Bring Jeanne Martinson to your community or organization for a half or full day workshop on the models contained in *Hemingway or Twain - Unleashing Your Author Personality*

Author Coaching
  a. Help in finding your Author Personality
  b. Assistance in moving through the steps of the Book Project Model
  c. Trouble shooting a book in process or a book that is stalled.

See www.wooddragonbooks.com for more details

Contact Info

Jeanne Martinson, MA
Diversity Strategist, Best-selling Author,
Professional Speaker

Website: **www.martrain.org**
Mobile: 1.306.591.7993
Office: 1.306.569.0388
Snail Mail: PO Box 1216,
Regina, Saskatchewan, Canada S4P2B4

Made in the USA
Charleston, SC
22 November 2015